ago

The Neon Signs of Service™

Getting to the Heart of the Matter in Customer Service

by
Holly Stiel ©2001

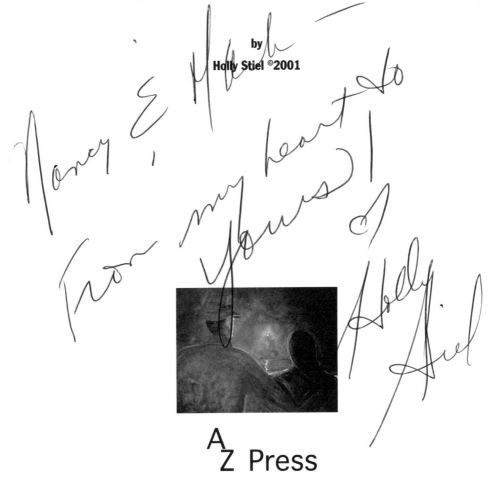

A
Z Press

Aptowitzer/Zvechtenstiel Press
An Old World Company With New World IDEAS

To contact the author with comments or to inquire about
speaking, seminars or consulting, email to:
thankyouinc.@aol.com

Book designed by Richard Bagel.

ISBN 0-9715370-03

Published by AZ Press
728 Bay Road
Mill Valley, CA 94941

Printed in the United States of America

The Neon Signs of Service™

Getting to the Heart of the Matter in Customer Service

by

Holly Stiel ©2001

"In service, a masterpiece is a person who arrives unhappy and leaves happy. But only an inspired and disciplined artist can create a masterpiece."

Holly Stiel

To *You*
A person who says, "How may I help you?"

It is my sincere hope that this book will be a source you will refer to many times. I suggest you read it through in its entirety and then go back to review as you put the "Neon Signs" into practice.

Remember, it is a practice and an art form. Have fun and thank you for the difference that you make.

Holly

Acknowledgements

Since this book is a compilation of many years of experience, there are many people to thank.

I appreciate all of the concierges and concierge associations who hired and supported me in presenting seminars and sharing the ideas I learned on the job. Most especially, Marjorie Silverman, Jerry Soh, Richard Ezekial, Inger Boudouris, Karim El Raheb, Michael Romei, Jeanne Jensen Perry, Diane Dillon, Jeff Larsen, Edward Munz, Louise Avery, Patty Doidge, Lorley Musiol, Tammi Furce, Nancy Green, Patti Dreisyzun, Gerry Parent, Marco Milanez, Rikako Ikeda, Naoki Kano, Laurie Gordon, Kate Anderson, Rob Alexander, Denyse McCoy, Dave Anderson, Pam Del Bosco, Rick Burton, Peter Rank, Leslie O'Brien, Brenda Verna, Virginia Casale, Miguel Pena, Vickie Apostolos, Ginny Thomason, Jim McCasland, Ron Palmtag and John Ruiz. Because of your support, I was able to hone my new craft and crystallize the ideas I am presenting in this book. A very special thank you goes to Diana Nelson and Maryann Smythe for being my partners in the learning process.

Thank you very much to the many supportive friends who have believed in these ideas: Nina Katz for giving me the opportunity to expand beyond the hospitality industry and introduce the "Neon Signs" to the banking industry. Pete Costner for being a visionary and exposing the security industry to hospitality. Louis Patler for helping me to make the transition from hotel concierge to the world of the entrepreneur. Bonnie Dean for her relentless positive praise. Dana Gribben for her brilliance and guidance as a coach and collaborator. Jana Stanfield for her love, support and precious friendship. Aimee Lyndon-Adams for her partnership, wisdom and the constant personal growth I experience in her presence. Nanci Sherman for her awesome applause. To Toni Boyle for her initial inspiration when she commented, "These Neon Signs are really good." I decided to write them down. To my fabulous friend and editor Barbara Christenson. We have realized the dream we visualized at the Lansing airport in 1995, as we casually said, "We could write a book together." Barbara, you truly are a goddess. Thank you very much!

Contents

Dedication

To my husband, Bill Apton, who makes everything possible (if I listed all the things that Billy does, it would be another book!). Thank you. I love you. You are my angel.

Preface

I slept and dreamt that life was joy.
I woke and realized that life was service.
I acted, and behold through service there was joy.
— Indigenous American proverb

Life constantly astounds me with its gentle nuances. The most pro-found lessons are so often found in unexpected places. I was caught totally off guard back in 1971, when I was doing my student teaching in Cincinnati, Ohio. An 8-year-old girl in a fourth-grade history class gave me my first lesson in customer service long before I had any idea I would build a career in it.

My first student teaching assignment was at the School for Crippled Children (this was in the era before the terms disabled and physi-cally challenged became politically correct). On my first day, I was invited to sit in the back of the room and observe.

There were fourteen students sitting in a semicircle at the front of the room, and it was time for a history lesson. The teacher asked for a volunteer to pass out the books. One little girl bounded from her chair to fill the request. No one else in the room was the least bit surprised that it was Susie.

You see, Susie didn't have any arms. As I watched incredulously, she walked to the book table, maneuvered two heavy books under her chin and walked purposefully to her classmates. Each child nonchalantly removed a book from under her chin. She repeated this seven times until each of the fourteen children received their book.

I learned more in that moment than I could ever hope to teach in an entire semester.

What, you might be asking, is the customer service lesson here? What it illustrates to me so beautifully are the three basic principles that must be in place for customer service to be delivered at all. They are *willingness, patience* and *understanding.* Without these, I can teach you the "Neon Signs of Service" until we're all blue in the face, but it won't do any good.

Willingness – Without willingness, nothing else matters. Many times it involves saying, "Yes, I'll do it," even when it may look like you don't have what it takes to get the job done.

Patience – Whew! Slow down. Stop, look and listen. F-l-o-w. Isn't this a concept we need in our hurry-up world? Front-line service tries your patience every day.

Understanding – Being open to the possibility that there is something to learn from everyone, even when they seem very different.

As a service provider, you need to be *willing.* Then, you must have *patience,* which is the temperament to serve. If you have those things, you can grow into the *understanding* that through service, a beautiful journey may unfold for you and all those you touch.

I learned how to see things differently through the gifts of special children.

This picture was a gift to me from my student during the first year I taught special education. She drew it with her feet.

The Neon Signs™

I didn't have any background in the hospitality industry when I became a hotel concierge in 1976.

I had arrived in San Francisco, armed with my Masters Degree in Special Education, and I can honestly say that it had never occurred to me that a teaching job could be difficult to get. Reality, however, was that in 1975, there were over 100 applicants for each job posting. After being rejected time and time again, I decided God must have another plan for me.

Looking around my chosen geographic location, I asked myself, what was happening in San Francisco that would interest me other than teaching? The answer came quickly — tourists! So I decided to seek out jobs that related to tourism. My first foray into that world was working for a company called "Smiling Faces" handing out brochures at trade shows and making name tags. Through a connection at Smiling Faces, I found out about a job working for a tour company in a hotel lobby. It sounded like fun, and as it turned out, that little tour desk in the lobby of the Hyatt on Union Square changed my life.

From the very first hour I worked behind that desk, I *knew* that it was my destiny, even though I had never heard of a concierge, let alone understood what the word meant. I can't explain the feeling. It was simply a knowing that I was in the right place at the right time. The rest, as they say, is history.

The 17 years I spent as chief concierge at the Grand Hyatt, the career in speaking and training that it spawned, and the integral role I have played in pioneering the concierge profession in America, began at a little desk in a big lobby with a lot of faith in my inner knowing.

Suddenly I was stationed in the center of the lobby of a 750-room hotel being relentlessly bombarded by questions. Now I did my best to get out of the lobby and actually learn what I was talking about — on my days off, I rode the cable cars, visited museums, took tours and pretty much pretended I was a tourist!

Whether guiding people inside or outside the hotel, I found that I was in the "helping" business. I was asking questions and seeking help from my sources to get answers to my customers' questions, as much as they were making requests of me. Consequently, it became my responsibility to be as thankful and courteous as I hoped my customers would be to me.

So my compass for each day became the magic words, "Thank You Very Much." If I wasn't hearing them and wasn't saying them all day, I realized something had gone terribly wrong. Those words became my barometer — the way that I measured the success of my workday. I'd have a competition — just with myself — to see how many times I could hear those magic words. I realized early on that the business I was really in was the "Thank You Very Much" business — the bottom line of every service interaction.

To make that concept come alive, I visualized a neon sign with "Thank You Very Much" flashing every time I heard the words. Then I imagined the words on my forehead. I could pull an invisible chain and the sign would go on!

This idea worked so well for me that as I developed other techniques for dealing with the daily rigors of serving the public, I automatically attached neon signs to them. When I started training people in my customer service philosophies and techniques, the individual signs became a group, and hence, this book!

Holly Stiel's Neon Signs of Service:

Stay in Touch with the Challenge
Choose
The "ME" Sign
Deal with the Double D's
It Isn't Personal
Forgive
Notice, Name and Choose
Being Right Is the Booby Prize
Look for the Love
Breathe and Stretch
The Wings of No
Apologize
Keep Dancing
Lights, Camera, Action
Bring Your Sense of Humor to Work
   Special Neon Signs
Thank You Very Much

There is a Sanskrit word Pra'jnapardha which means, "crimes against wisdom." It isn't enough just to *know* the wisdom. You must commit yourself to living it, acting on it and, just as importantly, forgiving yourself when you commit crimes against it.

The following pages are filled with "The Neon Signs" — the service wisdom that served me well during my 17 years on the front line. They're very simple reminders — anchors that will keep you on track and on purpose when you're tempted to go astray. They evolved out of real-world experiences and are guaranteed to serve the server as well as the customer. Putting these "Neon Signs" into practice will elevate the work you do to art — service as art.

THE NEON SIGNS OF SERVICE
Getting to the Heart of the Matter in Customer Service

The Psychic Salary™

Like most every other person who works, I worked at my job as a hotel concierge for a paycheck! Yet I was excited about the opportunity. I'm a people-pleaser, and here was an industry that gave me the opportunity to please and that had comment cards and instant feedback. Well, I quickly learned that I couldn't please all of the people all of the time. Still, I knew I *wanted* to please, as it made me *feel* good. Even with that attitude at the core, demanding people and relentless requests were taking their toll. To survive in this difficult world, and eventually thrive in it, I invented my very own "Psychic Salary."

While your actual paycheck, in monetary form, comes from an outside source, your "Psychic Salary" is an inside job.

> I was working as a consultant for a large firm in downtown San Francisco, when I encountered a parking attendant whom I will never forget. He exemplified a service provider who was into the essence of his job. He wasn't exactly singing and dancing, but he could have been. He was that courteous, warm and welcoming. It was as if it was his job to set up my day for me to be positive and upbeat. I had to interview him! When I asked him what inspired him, he told me he was the **ambassador** of the parking lot. That's what he believed . . . that's what he was! Everyone else working there was just parking cars.

Another case . . .

> One time I asked a bartender who was obviously dancing through his shift, how he viewed his job. He said, "I'm the swizzle stick that stirs the drinks." Whew! With an attitude like that, his shift flew by!

These people paid themselves a "Psychic Salary." Do you see the distinction? Your monetary paycheck is a contract. By cashing it, you've agreed to live by the rules and provide the service required. Your "Psychic Salary" is up to you! You get to pay yourself! It's a bonus! Without it, your paycheck is just a paycheck. With it, you're an ambassador or a fancy swizzle stick. The job function is the same.

So how do you shift to this frame of mind? The first step is to ask yourself this question: *"How does serving others serve you?"* What do you get out of your service job (besides the paycheck)? Is there another paycheck, a mental paycheck — a "Psychic Salary"?

In North America we have a service economy that for the most part does not honor service providers. If you're wearing a uniform and name tag, you may feel like a second-class citizen — sometimes because you are actually being treated that way and other times because of your own attitude.

Either way, that's what the "Neon Signs of Service" are all about — ways to earn your very own "Psychic Salary" (mental paycheck) through employing your own power to serve yourself while you're serving others. It is up to each of you individually to discover what the benefits of serving are for you personally.

You'll earn your "Psychic Salary" once you know the answer to the question: *"How does serving others serve you?"* Perhaps you enjoy working with a terrific team — playing your part in the success of the team, the big picture is important to you. Maybe helping others fulfills a deep-seated need to be needed — that was my motivating behavior. Possibly your job provides you with the opportunity to feed your self-esteem. It could be as simple as your desire to enjoy a pleasant environment. Restaurant workers have shared that they get their "Psychic Salary" from the socialization and party-type atmosphere often promoted in restaurants.

It makes no difference what the "Psychic Salary" is. What's important is that you're self-aware — you know why you are doing what you do.

Service can only come from one place — each individual service provider. It is created from the inside-out, not the outside-in. Understanding what is in it for you personally will give you the stamina you need to create and sustain a quality service environment and experience.

Once you know where your "Psychic Salary" is coming from, ask yourself "To what degree am I paying myself?" Fifty percent of the time, eighty, one hundred percent? Each day may be different and pay a different percentage. If you're not receiving any "Psychic Salary," perhaps it would be a good idea to reevaluate what you are doing and why you are there. There are many ways to get a paycheck — working with people is only one of them. If you choose to work with people, the value of a "Psychic Salary" is an absolute necessity. The more you are willing to view it that way, the larger your "Psychic Salary" becomes.

You earn your "Psychic Salary" when you pay attention to the essence of your job, in addition to the function. Your interactions with others are the key to your joy and success. When you understand that, you have a personal reason for providing good service, instead of because someone tells you to do it.

By concentrating on the humanity of people working with people instead of just the function of getting the task accomplished, you open up the possibilities for real satisfaction, and pride in your work experience. Can pride, satisfaction, self-esteem, and satisfying our deepest needs be measured? Do they have real value? I believe they do.

An elderly European guest handed me a telegram to send to his daughter in Israel. I told him we could send it first thing in the morning. To him, first thing meant literally first thing, as the next morning he arrived at my desk in a robe and slippers, telegram in hand!

> *I read the message, which had his flight number on it, and it was signed "see you sun." I asked if that would be see you Sunday? He responded with a very heavy accent and said no, it meant **soon**, see you sun!*

The humanity of that interaction has always warmed my heart and brightened my spirits. The function of my job was to send the telegram. The essence was to be in rapport with a lovely human being.

KEVIN THE FRUIT MAN
The King of the Psychic Salary

Kevin would readily admit that his demeanor is, well, offensive to some people. Actually, his appearance could be viewed as odd at best, and bizarre at worst. He is clean. However, I was never sure what color hair to expect — from a palette of purple, green, or orange — or where on his body a new "earring" might be protruding. I always drove quickly past the fruit stand he manned near my home in Mill Valley, CA.

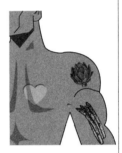

One day, convenience took precedence over my judgmental attitude. It was a very hot day, and Kevin was shirtless. This took his appearance to a new level — we're talking major tattoos, and they weren't hearts and snakes! They were fruit!!! Kevin's chest was emblazoned with an artichoke, a winter melon graced his back, and a zucchini ran the length of his left forearm.

I thought hmmm, this guy is *seriously* into fruits and vegetables! As I was purchasing my fruit, I mentioned to Kevin that I really love nectarines.

Three weeks later, I stopped again. This time Kevin was fully dressed and sporting hair the color of Pippin apples. I wasn't even out of my car, when he came running toward me with a beautiful, perfectly ripe nectarine in hand, shouting, "Killer nectarines, we have killer nectarines here today."

I was totally startled that he had remembered me, remembered my favorite fruit, and even remembered my car! I was so fascinated with his behavior and attitude that I impulsively asked him out to dinner! He was equally startled.

Being a student of customer service is what makes me a teacher. This guy fascinated me. I simply had to know what went on in his head. Why did he choose to do his job this way? He was not the owner of the fruit stand, and it certainly wasn't the glamour. So what was it?

A few days later I posed that question to him at dinner. By the way, Kevin is so thoughtful he dyed his hair black just for the occasion. What he told me confirmed the fact that Kevin was in touch with his "Psychic Salary." Kevin lived 45 minutes from the fruit stand, so everyday he rode his motorcycle across the Golden Gate Bridge to open the fruit stand, and every day during that 45-minute ride he psyched himself up with a statement he repeated over and over again: "You know Kevin, you can make a difference today, you can make a difference in someone's life today."

Now, it was making sense. The function of Kevin's job was to sell the fruit. The essence was to make a difference. Everyone who works with people has that opportunity. Kevin's "Psychic Salary" was to make a difference, and he earned it tenfold.

A few years ago, Kevin told me that a lady he'd never seen before had stopped by with a special message. It was from her mother who had just passed on from a terminal illness. On her deathbed she asked her daughter to please go and tell the fruit man "Thank You," because he had always made her feel so special.

If you believe your job and what you do makes a difference, then it does!

Service providers are so amazingly powerful. They have the opportunity to touch people's lives in meaningful ways. If, as a service provider, you are simply involved in the function of your job, you not only miss out on making a difference for others, you rob yourself of your own psychic salary.

The over-arching "Neon Sign" and theme of all the neon signs is that service is a challenge. Let's acknowledge that first. If you're tired of gritting your teeth while you're smiling, this book is for you.

THE NEON SIGNS OF SERVICE
Getting to the Heart of the Matter in Customer Service

Stay In Touch with the Challenge

Pull up this "Neon Sign" first, before all of the others: "Stay in Touch with the Challenge." Yes, service is a *challenge* and yes, you can *do it*. Rise to it! Be aware of it! Be *willing* to challenge yourself.

While the basic principles of customer service are painstakingly simple, they are not easy to perform consistently, and particularly under duress. "Staying in Touch with the Challenge" requires awareness, understanding and practice. The challenge is to get past the initial negative emotional triggers without getting stuck in them, and choose to serve by focusing on the task at hand and using empathy and caring with the customer.

"Staying in Touch with the Challenge" means taking ownership of your personal responsibility in every interaction. Each person has a responsibility to recognize that their actions, reactions and energy create their experience. Creating a zone of fun and hospitable service around yourself and your workplace is the responsibility and the challenge facing the service provider.

Positive energy doesn't just happen because some people are simply lucky — a positive outlook and energy field happen because of a conscious effort to make it so.

The same is true for negative energy. If we are emanating negative vibes, it is because we have chosen that path, most likely unconsciously. It is a challenge to make conscious choices, but in service we must rise to that challenge, lest we affect hundreds of others with a domino effect.

> *I was once in a deli near the San Francisco airport. I ordered a sandwich, and watched in horror as the woman who made it argued with a co-worker and actually snarled at me as well. The negative energy she put into making my sandwich put me off so much that I actually refused to buy it once it had been made. I said, "My moments are too precious to me, and I cannot ingest the negativity that you just put into my order," and left.*

The best we can possibly do is to be aware of our energy patterns, be able to handle the energy patterns of others, and stay present moment to moment. In the end, everything is energy.

I was walking through a casino property in Las Vegas on the way to give a seminar when I was struck by the wisdom in this sign:

You've got be present to win.

Another lesson learned in an unlikely place. "Staying in Touch with the Challenge" is staying present.

THE NEON SIGNS OF SERVICE

Getting to the Heart of the Matter in Customer Service

Choose

Every time the phone rings, every time the door opens or a customer approaches the counter, you have the opportunity to interface with a customer or colleague. Over and over again, you have the opportunity to "Choose." It is the constant underlying force of every action you take. Will you *stop and choose* or will you *unthinkingly choose*. Every other "Neon Sign of Service" wisdom depends on this one word, "Choose."

This simple word empowers you to take responsibility for your interactions and realize that the results of a customer's experience are almost always your choice. I use the word *almost* because there is very little involved in service that can be modified by the adverb, *always* — mostly there are shades of gray that these "Neon Signs" will help you to navigate.

This "Neon Sign" is so powerful it can magically transform a stressful situation in the blink of an eye.

On one very overwhelming day on the job, I had my head down staring at the computer, attempting to complete at least one item on my demanding list of priorities. I really needed some time and space to accomplish my tasks. I did not want to help one more person.

Instinctively, I felt the presence of yet another customer. I continued to look down at my computer screen, hoping against hope that by not acknowledging the customer, they wouldn't really be there. Seconds passed and I knew I had to not only acknowledge, but serve the person who had approached my desk. As I looked up, I flashed the neon sign *"Choose"* in my head and as the customer came into my field of vision I saw a most amusing picture — a man, about 5 feet 3 inches tall wearing a powder blue suit, a darker-color shade of blue shirt, and a different-color blue handkerchief.

> *He reminded me of a song my mother used to play when I was a child. It went "I wuv you, I wuv you, said the little blue man, and scared me right out of my wits." Immediately I said, "I love your suit!" He was delighted and I was tickled pink as well. By choosing to be in the present moment, I broke the tension and changed the energy, allowing me to help him with a smile on my face. I continued my multitasking in a much better frame of mind, all because I chose.*

It's up to you, moment by moment.

Throughout this book, you'll read about the opportunity to make choices — time and time again, knowing that you have the opportunity to make these choices is the saving grace of the customer service professional.

HOLLY'S LITTLE BLUE MAN

My artist husband painted this to cheer me up and to remind me of the power of choice.

THE NEON SIGNS OF SERVICE

Getting to the Heart of the Matter in Customer Service

The "ME" Sign™

The "ME" Sign is a sign within a sign. In customer service, very few things can be stated as absolutes, that is, without qualifications or exceptions. This "Neon Sign" is one of the absolutes. It is unequivocally a statement of truth. Recognizing and applying this fact of life in the world of customer service can revolutionize your daily work life. In a constantly changing world, this is a constant you can count on.

Every single customer that service providers will ever encounter wears a giant sign (this is true for you when you are a customer as well), and that sign says "ME." The sign has flashing lights all around it! In fact they are so bright, they temporarily blind the person wearing the "ME" sign. It is a reality of human nature.

I remember feeling incredulous when people would start speaking to me and demanding my attention, when I was already obviously on two telephones and in the midst of several tasks. My mind quickly went to, "Can't they see I'm on two phones?"

The answer is, no, they can't! The flashing lights of the "ME" sign are blinding them! In order to be successful in the service business, service providers must accept the indisputable fact of the "ME" sign's predominance and learn to become maestros in the "Me, Me, Me, Meeeeeeeee" orchestra!

Start by accepting it as unchangeable. It's the reality of every service business. Recognize that every customer wears one. And now here is the important part — you need to understand what is truly going on in the situation. What are the human needs behind the business at hand for all customers? What is the screaming "ME" sign really saying?

A former boss once told me that customers don't care about our problems. They only care about getting their needs met. He also said, "Customers rarely complain about price when they feel totally served."

A seminar participant relayed the following story:

> *While working a late shift as a room-service waiter, the chef on duty had a cardiac arrest. With the ambulance on its way, the waiter was fumbling to handle the orders himself. One customer was furious that her room-service order was so late. When the waiter explained that the chef had suffered a heart attack, her reaction expressed the very hot glow of a classic "ME" sign. "I'm not feeling very well myself, and I needed you to bring me what I ordered, right away!"*

While customers may appear different, every single one is wearing a "ME" sign. You meet customers who are friendly, others who are abrupt, or who have an "attitude" (more on this in a later chapter), yet they're all wearing "ME" signs. Behind the flashing lights of every "ME" sign are some universal truths. I call them the human needs behind the business needs. When service providers pay attention to these human needs, the business needs are easier to handle. As always, this requires *willingness, patience and understanding.*

The four human needs underlying every "ME" sign are *the need to be heard, the need to be acknowledged, the need to be remembered* and *the need to be respected.* When I ask seminar participants to relate a time they were served well, it *always* has these four elements. Service is intangible. It's all about perception and feelings. Only occasionally do people talk about job knowledge — the function of the job. That's a given. It's the intangibles that make the difference. Focusing on these four things will give you the tools you need to make people feel valued and important.

1 - People are screaming "ME" because they feel they haven't been heard. The first human need is to be *heard*, to be listened to. So listen intently, look for the key words in what people are saying. Lean forward, nod, and take notes if you choose. Really listen!

2 - The next human need behind the "ME" sign is the craving to be *acknowledged*. Notice me, make me feel important and pay attention to me. If I'm waiting in line, point at me, whisper "I'll be right with you," wink, do something that lets the "ME" know that you see me. In most cases it relieves the anxiety of the big "ME" sign. A simple acknowledgement works wonders.

3 - The third human need underneath the flashing "ME" sign is to be *remembered*. As I learned in the hotel business, nothing sounds sweeter than the sound of your own name. Remembering people's names and personal preferences is a primary factor in retaining loyal customers. To remember their last visit to a hotel, restaurant, or department store is to ensure a happy customer.

4 - The last human need behind the "ME" sign is *respect me*. Don't make me feel stupid. Appreciate that I am spending my time and money at your place of business and make me feel valued.

To be heard, acknowledged, remembered and respected.

This is the great challenge service providers face every day. The reality is, customers usually receive indifference. Therein lies the dilemma and source of the terrible service issues we have in North America. Herein lies the opportunity for you to make a difference.

A seminar participant shared this great story.

He is a concierge in Chicago. His hotel has come up with a very unique amenity — the opportunity to have a live goldfish in your room during your stay. One guest requested his goldfish through the housekeeping department. The request was not fulfilled. The next day he repeated the request, and again, no goldfish.

*At checkout, the guest expressed his displeasure at this oversight. Overhearing the conversation, the concierge immediately set into action the Neon Sign **"ME"** and took to heart the human needs **"to be heard, acknowledged, remembered and respected."** He called a concierge in the guest's home city, and arranged to have a goldfish delivered to his place of business the next working day. When the man got to work and saw a goldfish from the hotel, with a letter of apology, his **"ME"** sign lit up on all four circuits. He had been **"heard, acknowledged, remembered and respected."***

The following story is from a book that my father gave me on my 14th birthday. I have always attempted to live by this lesson.

THE OTHER FELLOW
By Clifton Fadiman
Writer and Lecturer

The worst sin toward our fellow creatures is not to hate them, but to be indifferent to them, that's the essence of inhumanity.
– George Bernard Shaw

Alone, no man can save himself. Alone, no man can find himself. Alone on his island, Robinson Crusoe was merely a highly ingenious animal. With the arrival of Friday, he became a man.

We cannot love all our fellow men, except in the most abstract way. But we can at least not be indifferent to them. We can cultivate awareness, we can try always to connect. What is civilization, after all? Surely it is man's effort to grow away from his original state of brutal separateness of indifference. It is the bridge one man throws up to connect himself with another man; the sense of connection is like a muscle. Unused, it withers. Exercised, it grows. Look at the next strange face you see, in a train, a theater lobby, behind a counter, really look at it. Behind those eyes there is a whole life, as complicated, as mysterious as your

own. If for only a fleeting instant, you can feel the pressure of that life, you have hailed in passing that unique miracle — the other fellow.

**From: *Words to Live By*
William Nichols, Editor
Simon & Schuster, 1959**

Have you ever noticed service providers who do everything correctly and nothing right? They wait on the customer, the words come out, the job gets done, but there is absolutely no connection. The job is simply about the mechanics. A little passion, a little love, changing the context of what the job is really about, understanding the "ME" sign, would open up the possibility for a connection, and it's a connection that people truly desire.

If the right words are simply the rote words, what good are they? To deadpan, "Welcome to Denver International Airport. We are glad you are here. We hope you had a nice trip. Thank you for choosing..." It's insulting, isn't it? If it sounds like a machine, it would be better to have a machine provide the service.

To be heard, acknowledged, remembered and respected requires a deeper response than a robotic, "Certainly, that would be my pleasure." You must sound like you really mean it or don't say it! Connect with the customer. Respond to their "ME" sign and chances are you'll enjoy an interchange with another human being resulting in a huge "Psychic Salary."

It's so simple. It's just not easy.

DEAL WITH THE DOUBLE D'S

THE NEON SIGNS OF SERVICE

Getting to the Heart of the Matter in Customer Service

Deal with the Double D's

I wish I didn't have to write this, but the truth of the matter is that I had to give these customers a name, so that we as service providers could make a quick I.D. of them. I call them the Double D's, meaning Demeaning and Disrespectful. It's so important to be aware of this, because their treatment of service providers (and people in general) is very hurtful. I will say that sometimes people just aren't thinking, sometimes they're in a bad mood and other times they're just plain rude. Regardless of the reason, the impact on service providers is the same.

These customers challenge your patience and could in fact break your service spirit. I want to make it very clear here that I am *not* talking about *abuse* — no one should be abused in service positions. Excessively foul language and physical threats are not appropriate and need not be tolerated. I submit that some customers should be fired! You can quote me on that.

This Neon Sign, "Deal with the Double D's," is for helping you cope with those customers who are annoying, push your buttons, and set up a feeling of resentment — the ones that make you think, "They don't pay me enough to put up with this," or "Why wasn't I born rich?" They're also responsible for sending you to fantasyland, where dreams of winning the lottery are set to the tune of, "Take this job and shove it!"

One morning, my associate Maryann Smythe was assisting a customer who had asked her to sew a button on his jacket. While this was not a common request of a concierge, Maryann was happy to do it as a gesture of goodwill. The demeaning aspect had nothing to do with being helpful and fixing the button. While she was sewing the button, the guest laid his briefcase on the desk, opened it, pulled out a can of spray deodorant and proceeded to spray deodorant under each arm, over the top of *his shirt — just a few feet from Maryann! Watching this incredulously, Maryann finished the task at hand, returned the jacket with the mended button and continued her shift. While the customer's performance was inappropriate, Maryann was clear that her job was simply to **"deal with it"** — accept the fact that all people are not cognizant of proper etiquette and move on.*

It was a perfect moment where her Neon Sign, "Choose" flashed, quickly followed by "Deal with the Double D's," followed by "It Isn't Personal."

Actually "Dealing with the Double D's" requires the use of another "D" word — *detach!* You must first detach from the situation at hand, become an observer, and immediately engage in choice.

Remember, I worked in the lobby of a 750-room hotel, answering 300 questions a day. By using this "Neon Sign," I learned to cushion myself from customer disrespect, to the point where I have become an observer of human behavior and quite frankly, have never found a more interesting or fascinating pastime! People are amazing, and when you can flow with it and laugh about it, you've mastered the *art* of service. Your success and your power are in your ability to choose.

A guest took a hundred-dollar bill from his wallet and tore it in half, handed it to my colleague and said, "If you're good, and get me the things I want, you get the other half."

Condescending? Demeaning? Only if you choose to see it that way.

*On his way back from jogging, a man who was dripping in sweat decided it would be a good time to ask me some questions. As his stench wafted across my desk, he dropped a ball of sweat all over my log sheets and Post-its. This was definitely a moment for **"Staying in Touch with the Challenge!"** I admit I was seething*

*inside for a moment. Then my **"Neon Signs"** came to the rescue: **"Deal with the Double D's," "Choose,"** and **"It Isn't Personal."** I chose to serve, and answered his questions!*

The odds are that only a small percentage of customers fit into the category of "Double D's" or any of the other personalities that might push your buttons. Therefore, my rule of thumb goes like this: If you experience three jerks in a row, take a break and look in the mirror. Maybe it's you! I call it "The Three Jerks in a Row Rule."

It is part of "Staying in Touch with the Challenge" to take responsibility for your actions. Is your behavior creating an environment that encourages customers to react in kind? In Psychology 101, I learned that the human response to stress is fight or flight. In the service business, those two options are not available! So, if you can't fight and you can't flee, it is important to learn to flow.

A few strategies for "Dealing with the Double D's":

♥ Repeat the mantra: "It Isn't Personal." Poor soul, he was so rude. I'm glad I don't have that life.

♥ Do not take on the negative energy of others. Literally use your hands and push away the other person's energy saying: "It isn't mine, I do not accept it." It is best to not do this in front of the customer; be discreet. Just make sure you don't take it on. Remember — it's your choice.

♥ Go to a health food store and purchase tinctures and homeopathic remedies with humorous names like Anger and Resentment drops. They actually do calm you down, and just the thought of using them can make you smile.

 Delivering excellent service consistently requires high self-esteem. When other people try to degrade you, remember that they can't do that without your permission.

This is when inner strength, personal power, and self-reliance are all-important qualities to draw on. When people treat you in demeaning and disrespectful ways, what they are really saying is that they don't feel good about themselves. Therefore, a positive self-image is a requirement when "Dealing with the Double D's."

The Double D's happen. Our job is to deal with it.

THE NEON SIGNS OF SERVICE
Getting to the Heart of the Matter in Customer Service

It Isn't Personal

What an amazing concept this is! Is it really possible to deliver personal service, to give of yourself, to take pride in your work and still believe that when a customer is yelling, complaining, or being overly aggressive that it is *not* a personal attack?

I believe that it is! Unless someone knows you personally, they cannot possibly be referring to you as a person. They are simply reflecting their feelings about the company, the situation, and their own way of processing frustration and undelivered expectations. It is all about them and very little about you! This is absolutely the best technique, tool and strategy for "Dealing with the Double D's."

I first learned this very valuable, albeit difficult lesson from Mac, one of the senior bellman at the Grand Hyatt. I was a fresh-faced rookie in the hospitality business, still in the "reacting" mode of letting my personal feelings rule every situation.

I watched in utter disbelief as a guest snapped his fingers at Mac with the words, "Boy, take my bags to my room." Mac responded with, "Certainly, sir, I'm right behind you."

When Mac returned from the guest's room I couldn't wait to talk to him. "How on earth did you respond the way you did? Didn't you want to smack the guy?" I asked Mac incredulously.

"It isn't personal," Mac said. "It wasn't about me." Ohhhhh! My goodness, what a concept! I never forgot his answer and it saved my sanity hundreds of times.

To deliver personal service and yet not take things personally is the ultimate balancing act. It is the flying trapeze in the service circus.

If a customer is upset and venting, they don't care to whom or what they are venting. At that moment, they are a "venting machine." If you're the object of their wrath, just remember that if it were your day off, they'd be yelling at someone else. It's not about you on a deep personal level.

CAVEAT: It may *feel* personal.
That is where the challenge is! You must:

"Stay in Touch with the Challenge"
"Choose"
"Deal with the Double D's"
and believe, "It Isn't Personal"

Now, the issue may in fact be about your job performance or someone else's, or their perception of it based on their level of expectation. However, the application of this "Neon Sign" is the same. By understanding that "It Isn't Personal," you can respond by acting responsibly instead of emotionally.

*My experience at the concierge desk during my hotel career illustrates this **"Neon Sign"** beautifully. My long-time associate, Maryann Smythe, is a very thin, angular blonde. I am a brunette and would never, even in my best dreams, describe myself as very thin. Guests confused the two of us consistently! They would say, "I talked to you yesterday for 20 minutes." Yet, it couldn't have been me — I was off that day! So much for taking it personally!*

In one of my seminars, a participant (mid-level manager) told me this story.

She had volunteered to check coats for a large banquet that a local Boston charity was holding at the hotel. While taking the coats from two guests, the father said to his daughter in a very loud voice, "This is why you have to go to college. If you don't, you could end up like her."

Now this is a perfect example of "Dealing with the Double D's," — not taking it personally. It may have been demeaning. It may have been disrespectful, but it wasn't personal!

EXERCISE:

Can you think of a time you reacted personally and emotionally to something a customer said or did that you realize now wasn't personal?

IDEA:

Create a support circle at work. You can do this in small groups of three or four or with just one other person.

Each person takes two or three minutes to speak out loud about a time they were demeaned or treated disrespectfully at work. The others do nothing but listen supportively (no comments). After the story, the supporter(s) say out loud:

"It Isn't Personal"

THE NEON SIGNS OF SERVICE

Getting to the Heart of the Matter in Customer Service

The *NEW* Neon Sign: "Forgive"

I had an epiphany recently. I was working with my partner Aimee, designing a two-day class on front-line customer service using all the "Neon Signs," these simple, yet profound truths based in the age-old wisdom of kindness, gratitude, love and humor. We were talking about dealing with customers that "push your buttons" when Aimee suddenly went off on a tangent and started talking about old hurts and the personal power and benefit that forgiveness can bring to them.

It seemed to both of us that this diversion was somehow on target with the work we were doing, when suddenly that wonderful "Aha!" moment occurred . . .

    i.e., Think ...   **And say ...**

In an instant I realized that the exact thing I had been teaching is responsible for one of the biggest gaps in quality service. That is, there's a lack of congruency between what people are thinking and their actual behavior. The *truly effective* strategy is to add an element of forgiveness to the mix of emotions that surface when faced with a rude, demanding, demeaning or panicked customer.

Flash!

"Stay in Touch with the Challenge"
"Choose"
"Deal with the Double D's"
"Forgive"
"It's Not Personal"

Yes, that's right, forgive the customer for their behavior. Forgive them, then and there, in the moment. This is a key strategy to earning a "Psychic Salary."

Now that we have entered the new millennium, the concept of forgiveness has actually become newsworthy. "Good Morning America" devoted three days to segments on forgiveness ranging from the most heinous crimes to an unfaithful spouse. The findings were remarkable. In every case, the act of forgiveness proved to be the single biggest factor in healing the victim. There are now institutes devoted to forgiveness, classes in universities, a nonprofit association called Campaign for Forgiveness Research, and scientific testing on the ways forgiveness affects blood pressure, as compared to a revenge response. In every case, stress levels and blood pressure went down when people were willing to forgive others.

Forgiveness is a gift for you as well as the customer. It is something you are giving of yourself to the other person and it benefits you in the process. While forgiveness doesn't mean you forget — the power of forgiveness can be seen in the following illustration.

A seminar participant gave me this profound equation. What's the same in these two words: forgive and forget? The "for." Cancel out the "for" in each word, and you are left with "Give equals get." It makes sense to me!

To forgive in the customer service context — to forgive the customer for their behavior in the moment — should be the easiest type of forgiveness to master. After all, we have already established that "It Isn't Personal," so you should have no personal stake in holding on to negative thoughts.

Acknowledge them of course, and then "Choose." If you *choose* forgiveness, it will open up the space for you to actually serve. It will close the gap between attitude and behavior being so far apart. When you think one way and attempt to act in a service-oriented way, it always comes across as stiff and insincere. Customers are human lie detectors — they know if you are serving genuinely or not. If you can manage your emotions, and open your heart and mind to forgiveness you will be pleasantly surprised by the results.

We are constantly producing an electromagnetic field which affects the way people respond to us. Imagine the difference in energy when forgiveness becomes your strategy of choice.

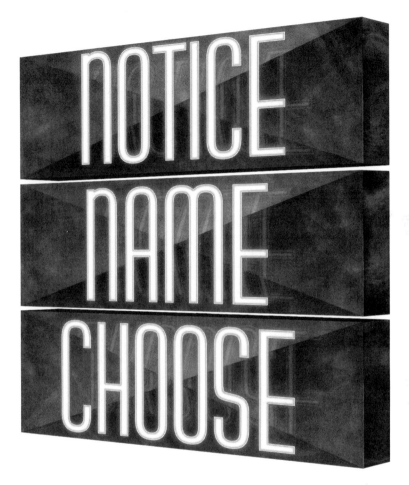

THE NEON SIGNS OF SERVICE

Getting to the Heart of the Matter in Customer Service

Notice, Name and Choose

It is not terribly challenging to be nice to nice people. Quite frankly, that is a no-brainer. What is challenging is to be nice to and *choose* to serve people you may find annoying. Therein lies the true challenge of serving people.

The best service providers, even those most dedicated to helping others, can be challenged by the small percentage of customers who quite simply push their hot buttons. When I talk about this in my seminars, I get a universal response. The same customers are pushing the same hot buttons all around the world! Everybody recognizes them. I've found it to be true in businesses as diverse as financial planning and corporate security.

I find it fascinating that while all customers wear a "ME" sign, only a small percentage exhibit attitudes that trigger negative emotions and push our buttons. Most seminar participants say the percentage of customers that push their buttons is very small, somewhere between three and ten percent. While in a large company this constitutes a large number of customers, it is nonetheless a small *proportion* of any customer base. That's where the danger lies. It is these customer attitudes, this small percentage, that break the service spirit of front-line service providers and have a crossover effect on the customer base that is perfectly delightful to serve. Three percent affect the remaining 97%!

EXAMPLE: Have you ever personally been a part of the 97% of a perfectly delightful customer base? Perhaps you've been waiting in line at a bank when you witness a situation where a customer is venting his rage on the teller. Eventually the difficult customer leaves and it is your turn. The upset and frustrated teller looks up, nods and says "Next." You are suddenly a victim of the three percent. If the teller had made use of the "Neon Signs," the chances of him/ her responding to the next person in line with a sincerely felt, "Good afternoon, may I help you?" are seriously increased.

These people arouse what I call negative emotional triggers. You just stop in your tracks and are taken aback. It's like a bell goes off, and your own energy turns negative. My solution is a formula I learned from Dana Gribben, a talented communications coach I worked with. I had done it naturally all the years I was at the Hyatt. It's called, "Notice, Name and Choose." It is actually a ten- to fifteen-second process.

(1) NOTICE:

Notice that you are having an emotional reaction. *Stay aware* of the emotional reactions you are experiencing. Some clues are short or shallow breathing, voice tone goes up a notch, and body tension significantly increases. Most people can actually feel a chemical change in their bodies (however, you've been taught to ignore it or work over it).

(2) NAME IT:

Give it a name. *Own your feelings.* This is not a strategy based on denying the truth. It is a strategy based on *owning* what is real for you, owning *your own feelings.* Name the initial gut reaction which feels bad, i.e., frustration, anger, "How dare you!" etc. Be aware enough of your own personal reactions to track how it might change from hurt to anger in a matter of seconds. Become a person who is an observer of self by observing the variety of behaviors that you may feel the urge to do out of anger, annoyance or dismissal.

(3) CHOOSE:

Choose to move beyond all the possible responses that represent the "low road" (the automatic tendency where everyone loses) and take a different road, one that will lead you to a large payoff in "Psychic Salary," health, and increased energy. Choose the "high road" response. The high road response includes forgiveness and leads to service and satisfied customers. Best of all, it is a place where everyone wins. Your success and power is truly in your ability to choose.

When service providers master this skill, the company's service levels escalate, as does the self-esteem of service providers. Rising above these negative emotional triggers will make you feel absolutely triumphant. If you don't learn to do this, you'll be dragged down by experiences like this one:

While working an evening shift, I got so stuck in a negative emotional trigger that my reaction even surprised me. A guest requested to dine at a very popular restaurant, and it was completely full. I suggested other comparable establishments, and apologized for the disappointment. This customer was determined to get what he wanted. I watched in horror as he actually had a childlike tantrum complete with stamping his feet and literally wailing in a crybaby voice, "But that's what I want." I have to admit, I lost my service focus with this person, and responded with a stern, "Stop whining!" The moment the words were out of my mouth, I wished I could take them back, but it was too late. The damage had been done. I got sucked into the negative trigger.

Whenever I tell this story in speeches or seminars, people inevitably come up to me and want to know what happened. Well, I was so shocked by my own behavior, that I started talking *really, really* fast, telling him about a restaurant that he would like better. I made him the reservation, gave him a confirmation card and he left. Then I arranged for the restaurant to deliver a complimentary dessert at my expense. CAVEAT: I certainly don't recommend that you ever tell customers to stop whining. I do, however, suggest that you stay aware of what pushes your buttons so you don't simply *react* to the negative emotional trigger.

The Attitudes

During my career as a hotel concierge, I became aware of certain behavior and attitudes in customers that repeated themselves continuously. These attitudes fascinated me not only because they appeared consistently, but also because they aroused the feelings that "push the buttons" of front-line service providers, including myself, and subsequently produced behavior that didn't serve my customers or me.

Being aware of the attitudes that push your buttons is the first step toward practicing the following "Neon Signs of Service":

"Staying in Touch with the Challenge"
"Choose"
"Deal with the Double D's"
"It Isn't Personal"
"Forgive"
"Bring Your Sense of Humor to Work"
"Being Right Is the Booby Prize"
"Thank You Very Much"

There are six characters* who represent the attitudes that pushed my buttons when I was on the front line, until I learned to *live* the "Neon Signs." I'm sharing them with you so that you can use them as signposts. The next time they appear as one of your customers, you can notice (stay aware), name (own your feelings), and choose to serve.

---

* There may be other characters that surface in your place of work. Another common challenge in banks, restaurants and department stores is the Lonely Hearts — folks who are lonely and simply need to talk.

These attitudes are, however, so universal that many people in my seminars call out a name saying, "Mrs. _____, she was just here last week!"

> **Disclaimer: If these attitudes appear to be feminine in orientation, that's just because I am a woman! They definitely cross gender lines.**

When I talk with clients about this part of my presentation, they are sometimes hesitant about portraying their customers in a "negative" light. Interestingly enough, this is absolutely *not* about focusing on the negative. Reality is that when we don't acknowledge and learn how to deal with these situations truthfully, the negativity becomes the focus and spreads to all customers, permeating everything. The antidote is "The Neon Signs." By practicing them faithfully, you will learn to be a master in the art of service.

At the end of this chapter we will discover the human needs behind the business needs which will assist you in your ability to serve. *Remember, we are not talking about abuse — no one should be abused by customers. This is about annoying, difficult and challenging attitudes.*

Another interesting thing to note: Most of us have not only served this type of customer, we have *been* this customer.

Attitude No 1: The Entitled

This attitude reeks of "I deserve!"

"I expect you to do this, you owe me this privilege, I am a good customer."

The energy it sends out is, no one else exists, and you have nothing else to do but to help them. Stay aware — the negative emotional trigger that "The Entitled" elicits is *resentment*. If you are aware of that emotion, you can choose to forgive in the moment. If you are not aware and simply have a hair-trigger response, the dangerous thought that quickly follows is this:

"Oh really! Well, just exactly who do you think you are?" The subsequent behavior that the danger thought leads to is an unwillingness to give of oneself to help such a customer. It inhibits problem solving and in essence, paralyzes the opportunity to provide service.

Attitude No 2: The Panicked

This attitude is overwhelming, tense, intense and *in your face*. It is fraught with fear and anxiety. This attitude screams of "ME" and is usually accompanied with a heightened tone of voice, and perhaps a sigh or two.

"What do you mean my order isn't ready?"

"You promised me I would have this."

"This is insane! I have to have this now. I'm late! I'm in a hurry. Do something!"

Stay aware. The negative emotional trigger that "The Panicked" can elicit is *protection*. You want to protect yourself from the onslaught of negative energy. If you are aware of that hair-trigger response, you could choose to forgive the panicked person in the moment and make efforts to solve their problem, calm them down, etc.

However, when you let the hair-trigger response run you, the danger thought that quickly follows is, "Oh great, now your problem has become my problem." The subsequent behavior that the danger thought leads to is for service providers to set up rigid boundaries that often result in a refusal to cross the boundaries necessary to perform problem-solving and service tasks.

Attitude No. 3: I'm Better Than You

The "I'm Better Than You" attitude may or may not come with finger snapping, but it is always demeaning in nature. This attitude dismisses service employees as nameless, faceless people just there to do their bidding. It looks down on anyone who wears a nametag and says without saying, "I'm better than you, and I'm not going to let you forget it." This attitude says, "Don't you know who I am — I know more about this job than you do. This better be good because I'm an aficionado!"

Stay aware — the emotional trigger that "I'm Better Than You" elicits is *shame and intimidation*. But to feel so belittled can quickly turn to anger, which is why this customer attitude is so danger-ous. It feels more personal than the others; therefore, it may be harder to forgive in the moment. It is possible though. Awareness and choice are the keys. If not, the danger thought that the anger and resentment might lead to is, "I'll show you." The subsequent behavior it leads to is revenge. In such a scenario, orders may get misplaced, diners end up at tables near the kitchen door and hotel guests get the room right next to the ice machine.

Attitude No. 4: Cut to the Chase

This attitude goes straight to the bottom line. These people are totally uninterested in schmoozing and friendliness. They want what they want. They are interested in efficiency only, or so it would appear.

"Can you do this for me, yes or no?"

"Tell me exactly when I can expect an answer."

"Your friendliness is getting me nowhere."

"What do you mean you'll do your best? Either you can or you can't."

Stay aware. The negative emotional trigger that the "Cut to the Chase" attitude elicits is *hurt and defensiveness.* The negative actions it can trigger and evoke are matching behavior. If customers can speak to service providers in a clipped and brusque manner, then why can't I (the service provider) talk to the customer in the same way? Unfortunately, that will only lead to a brief and usually negative response that has very little to do with quality service delivery.

Attitude No. 5: The Clueless

These are the customers that are not only totally unaware of how business operates; they seem clueless regarding anything having to do with common sense. They say things like,

"Huh?"

"If I go outside and it is raining, will I get wet?"

One of my friends was asked if the Canadian flag came in any other colors.

Stay aware. The negative emotional trigger that "The Clueless" elicits is *irritation*. If you are aware of that emotion, you can choose to forgive these customers in the moment. You can stay out of judgment and stay in touch with your purpose, that of taking care of customers — all kinds of customers. If you are not aware, and do not choose to forgive in the moment, the danger thought that quickly follows your initial trigger of irritation is this: "Why should I bother explaining anything to this person? He or she won't understand it anyway." The subsequent behavior that the danger thought often leads to is outright dismissal of the individual who is supposed to be served. All of these negative emotional triggers, danger thoughts, and subsequent behaviors prevent you from seeing the true agenda and makes it difficult to really serve people in a way that meets their needs.

Attitude No. 6: The Imprisoned

"The Imprisoned" are the people who are constantly whining and complaining. They say things such as,

"Why does something always go wrong?"

"Nothing ever works out for me."

"My whole trip has been like this, one disaster after another."

They are so imprisoned by their own misery that their only purpose in life seems to be to make other people miserable. "The Imprisoned" usually have such negative energy that things seem to go wrong for them on a consistent basis.

Stay aware. The negative emotional trigger "The Imprisoned" elicits is *frustration.* If you are aware of your own hair-trigger response of frustration, you can choose to forgive them. Try repeating a quote from my book, *Thank You Very Much,* to yourself: "Poor soul, I'm so glad I don't have his life."

The danger thought that quickly follows on the heels of the frustration is, "If you hate doing business here so much, why don't you take it elsewhere," — not the kind of thing you want your boss hearing you thinking!

The subsequent behavior this type of thinking leads to is very insincere and cold service. Service providers may go through the motions, but the customer will never feel served.

Here's how some of these attitudes show up in different industries:

The Entitled shows up . . .
- In banks when people don't want to pay a fee.
- In airlines when people expect an upgrade.
- In hotels, "But you gave me a suite last time I was here."
- In restaurants, "I want the best table and I don't want to wait."

The Panicked shows up . . .
- In hotels when people are late for a meeting, when packages don't arrive and messages get lost.
- In banks and other financial institutions when escrow doesn't clear, or a deposit is not entered.
- In airlines with missed connections and cancelled flights.
- In dry cleaners when clothes are stained or destroyed.
- In restaurants when people are in a huge rush.
- In parking garages, when they can't find their car — or their keys!

The I'm Better Than You shows up . . .
- Anywhere, everywhere — in hotels, banks, restaurants, airlines, parking garages, department stores, the dry cleaners. This is most often a look or a physical communication, rather than verbal.

Cut to the Chase shows up . . .
- In dry cleaners, "Can you remove this stain (now!)?"
- In banks, "Can I get the loan or not?"
- In hotels, "Can you type this for me in 15 minutes?"
- "Is someone on the way up here to fix my light, yes or no?"

The Clueless shows up . . .
• In hotels in the lobby in a strange city — they may not even know what hotel they're in, let alone the city!
• In banks, "But I still have checks."
• In the "10 items or less lane" at the grocery store, with 20 items.
• At the car rental, "And how do I get there?" when you just handed them a map and directions.

The Imprisoned shows up . . .
• In financial institutions when people complain about not getting their statements on time and not getting calls returned.
• In restaurants, "Not as good as it used to be." "Portions too small." "Not hot enough." "Not fast enough."
• In hotels, "Not friendly enough." "Waited too long for an elevator." "Don't like décor."
• In airlines, "Never on time." "Not enough space." "Hate the selection of food and movie."
• In department stores, "Don't like the dressing rooms, the layout, the colors this season."

(Some of these complaints may indeed be legitimate. "The Imprisoned," however, seem to only dwell on everything negative.)

How do these attitudes show up in your business? Are you willing to notice (stay aware), own your own feelings, forgive and choose to serve by taking the high road?

To help you in choosing the high road, remember:

"Stay in Touch with the Challenge"

"Choose"

and

"Forgive"

One thing is certain: these attitudes are not going to go away. They are human nature and are here to stay. What you *can* change is how you choose to respond. As a service provider, your power and your success lie in how you choose to respond to these attitudes. This is where the true challenge of service really lies. It's easy to be nice to people you enjoy. It is much more challenging, interesting, and rewarding to give quality service experiences to that small percentage of customers that push your buttons and may cause you to respond in a less than stellar way.

Remember the "ME" sign? It is even more important to focus on the human needs behind the business needs with this small percentage of customers.

Let's see what the human needs are for each of these customers. I thought it would be a good idea to ask them. What is the person really communicating by this behavior? What do they really need? Certainly not for the service provider to simply go through the motions of getting the job done.

What do I really want/need from you, the service provider?

• The Entitled

"I am really actually rather insecure. I don't know any other way to get what I want, so I act pushy. Getting special treatment is really important to me because I need to feel important. Would it be so difficult for you to make me feel important? Believe it or not, you have the power to do that. I hate to admit it, especially to you, but you hold the power to make or break my day. You see, I'm quite bored and often lonely. Please forgive me for my behavior, and help me to feel special and important. It will be better for both of us. I crave attention. That's why I act this way. Give me the attention I crave and I'll calm down."

• The Panicked

"Help me! I'm freaked out! I am beside myself. I am not acting like myself — I am scared and upset. I have a one-track mind at this moment, and I know I have blown everything out of proportion. The one thing I don't need you to do is to tell me to calm down. I need you to match my urgency, understand my situation — forgive my aggressive behavior and take over. I need reassurance; at this moment I feel powerless and out of control. This is so very uncomfortable for me, please help me."

• I'm Better Than You

"I cannot see past your function, so I have no idea who you are and what your value as a human being is. I am self-centered and look down on you to make me feel better. I am not even aware I am doing this. It isn't personal to you. I do this to everyone. Acting superior covers up all the things I don't want to see about myself. I need you to reinforce me, not try to teach me a lesson. I am the way I am and I don't want to change. I want you to understand that and not take it personally. I am only thinking about me."

• Cut to the Chase

"I am so overwhelmed by my own busy life that I have created a brick wall between myself and other people. I'm really hungry for a warm interaction, but I have no idea how to initiate it. I am in a constant hurry and have big responsibilities, so I desperately need you to be efficient. I also secretly need you to be warm and helpful as well. Could you forgive me for being so brusque? It's just that I don't know how to be any other way. I want your respect, and I think if I am all business, that I'll gain respect. Please get the job done quickly, but acknowledge and respect me in the process even if it appears that I am not doing the same for you. I am so tightly wound, I have no room for compassion."

• The Clueless

"I am very confused right now. I am out of my comfort zone. I don't understand how your business works. Maybe I'm not as bright as you, but I'm still your customer so please don't make me feel like more of an idiot than I already do. You have so much power over me, you can make feel stupid or you can make me a learning partner. Please forgive me for being what you might consider to be stupid, and help me to understand. You may have said the directions hundreds of times, but it is the first time I am hearing them. I need patience, I need kindness; please give me those things and don't make me look foolish."

• The Imprisoned

"Can't you see how miserable I am? I don't know how to act any other way. I've become accustomed to complaining about everything for so long now it has become my natural way of being. Please forgive me, and just let me vent. I'm just looking for some attention — someone to listen to me. At least empathize with me. Tell me you are sorry for my inconvenience and make an attempt to do something. I'm desperate for somebody to care, could you be that somebody?"

It helps to see things through someone else's eyes, doesn't it? This requires making some room in *your* "ME" sign. One of the major problems in service is that the service provider is wearing a "ME" sign, too. The customer is not going to take their "ME" sign off, so it is the responsibility of the service provider to dim the flashing lights on their personal "ME" sign.

When you respond by choosing to provide a quality service experience beyond your own personal barometer, then *The Entitled* is made to feel important and the center of attention. *The Panicked* is helped to feel assured and comfortable. *I'm Better Than You* is showered with compliments. *Cut to the Chase* experiences clarity. *The Clueless* is handled with patience. *The Imprisoned* experiences empathy.

To choose to do this requires that in each situation you ask yourself, "What does this customer really need and how am I going to provide it?" What is the human need that can be addressed, as opposed to just going through the motions and providing the business need? It's all about caring — emanating the essence of "I care." That's your responsibility as a service provider who is mastering the art of service.

I have a strategy for achieving this. I call it putting on the "Turtle Hat of Service." Most people don't think of a turtle relative to customer service (unless it's s-l-o-w service), yet the turtle is a wonderful metaphor for service. Once you have put on the turtle hat of service you can be reminded that service is a verb (an action word) and requires that you stick your neck out! The turtle hat also reminds you:

❤ That you need to learn to have a hard shell and not take everything so personally.

❤ The turtle hat also helps you to remember to slow down and not react so quickly to your negative emotional triggers and traps.

BEING RIGHT IS THE BOOBY PRIZE

THE NEON SIGNS OF SERVICE

Getting to the Heart of the Matter in Customer Service

Being Right Is the Booby Prize

It's been more than twenty years since the topic of customer service hit the bookstores and the lecture circuit. There is no shortage of verbiage and statistics on the subject, and there is plenty of negative press when the service is truly bad. What's really disturbing is that there are only a handful of businesses that consciously offer a sincere helping hand. How can that be, with all this information and training going on? It's really quite simple. Human behavior is the culprit. You see, human beings like to be right.

There is so much passion and personal feeling involved in both aspects of the service relationship — the customer as well as the service provider — that people will go to great lengths to protect themselves from what they feel are injustices. It is an automatic human response — the need to be right takes over, and the purpose of your job as a service provider takes a secondary position. So, as you can see, both "sides" become involved in being right and a no-win situation surfaces. "Being Right" is prized over outcome, process and reason, when in reality, "Being Right Is the Booby Prize." Talk about "Staying in Touch with the Challenge" — nothing is more challenging than this, and nothing is more rewarding. When you realize what is going on and "Choose" to forgo "Being Right," you are truly "Staying in Touch with the Challenge."

Most of the time the need to be right plays out in subtle ways, in little digs, choices of words, and the misguided notion that people *should* know better. While I am passionate about all the wisdom I share in this book, this "Neon Sign" is truly my personal favorite. It is the behavior behind most service breakdowns. Therein lies the power of its potential.

CAVEAT: There may be times when being right involves safety and security. Remember, nothing is *always*.

When the Neon Sign flashes, "Choose," you can choose to be right or you can choose to serve. You may be tested mightily.

One Saturday afternoon, I was working with a group of 14 "adults" visiting San Francisco from Los Angeles. They were celebrating a 40th birthday and they told me they had their heart set on a certain restaurant in the village of Sausalito (just north of San Francisco over the Golden Gate Bridge). It is a small restaurant, and they're not geared for accommodating large groups.

I intervened, and did what any well-connected, pride-filled concierge would do. I called the owner of the restaurant at his home on Saturday afternoon to plead their case. As a favor to me, he took the reservation for the birthday celebration. I was ecstatic, as I knew I had really contributed to their special weekend. The next morning, a Sunday, I arrived at work at 7 a.m. The note that greeted me created a surge of nausea, which quickly turned to fury.

*I was beside myself. I was lunging toward the phone when PJ, my associate, intervened. She literally had to physically hold my arms back while adamantly referring to the sign hanging over my desk — **"Being Right Is the Booby Prize."***

"Did you write this?" she asked.
"Yes," I responded. "But not in this case!"

*Very carefully, PJ brought me to my senses. She pointed out that it **did** apply to this case, as my primary relationship was with the restaurant — **"Staying in Touch with the Challenge"** — and no matter what I might say to the guest, the damage had been done. My job was to make it right with the restaurant — **"Choose"** — and not to make the guest wrong, although they clearly had trespassed on my integrity!*

The customer is not always right; however, they are always the customer. At that very moment, in the midst of that dreadful experience, I learned a very important service lesson.

I t is not your job as a service provider to teach people who have made it to middle age how to behave.
Your real job is to *go inside, notice what is happening, name and choose.*

I am very clear that this is *not* the easiest thing to do. It is, however, the path to success in service. The tendency for most people is to scold the customer. Or if you are astute enough not to scold, the alternative course of action is manipulation.

The manipulation phone call would go something like this: "Are you all right? I was so worried about you. The restaurant called to say you didn't make it. After your enthusiasm yesterday I was sure something terrible had happened. I knew people like you would never not show up after I disturbed the restaurant owner at home and asked for a special favor just for you."

Guilt, shame, and blame — it all boils down to a hypothetical slap on the wrist. *"Bad customer"* is the message. The customer gets it, no matter how you do it. What good does that do? Absolutely none!

I learned other things that day as well. I learned to take a credit card number as a security deposit for a large party's reservation. (So as not to keep you wondering, I went to the restaurant with flowers and mea culpa, and the relationship was saved. I never saw or spoke to anyone from that group of 14 again.)

Sometimes being right is so ingrained and so subtle we have no idea that is what we are doing.

> *A bellman in Reno told me a man handed him a dollar and said, "Go get an education."*

Stop. Freeze frame. "Choose." What are the choices the bellman had at that moment? He could be thinking, this guy is a jerk. He could have accepted the dollar, flashed the Neon Sign that said, "Deal with the Double D's" and "It Isn't Personal" and moved on to "Being Right Is the Booby Prize" or he could have chosen a different response that would make him right, and confirm that the person was being rude! Unfortunately, that is the response he chose. He said, "I do have an education. Keep your money." Did he win in the long run? I don't think so.

In a seminar for the banking industry, a participant came to see me after class. She took issue with this "Neon Sign" and relayed the following story.

> *The bank was very, very busy, and a very impatient customer pounded on her desk and said, "I demand an apology." (In the hotel industry this is an easy request. We simply apologize, delighted to fulfill the request so easily and inexpensively!) I asked her how she responded and she said "Sir, I am terribly sorry that we are so busy." Try as I might, I could not get her to see that her response was **not** an apology, it was being **right**. Apologizing is to say, "I'm so sorry about the wait." That is **"Staying in Touch with the Challenge,"** and **"Choosing"** to serve rather than **"Being Right."***

And, here's my own experience, as a customer!

One time I called a hotel company in Jamaica on December 23rd. The operator explained that because of the holiday, everyone was off and would return December 26th. On the 26th of December I called again. This time I was told that it was a holiday, and no one was available. Not wanting to be wrong, I repeated what I had been told on my previous call. The operator said, "No one would have told you that." In essence she was calling me a liar, and I had to wonder why was it so important for her to be right about this? I said that indeed someone had told me this and she said, "That must have been the guard, you know, G.U.A.R.D. — guard." Now I wasn't just a liar, I was a stupid liar. Wow, what an investment she had in being right. Could she have felt good about the exchange? I know I didn't. While initially it may be a momentary pleasure to be right, in the end everyone loses. Because. . .

"Being Right Is the Booby Prize"

<u>There's a bonus in this "Neon Sign." Giving up the need to be right is a timesaving technique!</u> In our overachieving society, Franklin Planners™, Day-Timers™ and other such systems rule our lives. Prioritizing, balancing, and organizing one's schedule is the subject of countless books and seminars. The crunch for time seems to be a malady of the late 20th century, while the gift of time is a valuable commodity. Letting go of the need to be right can actually buy you treasured moments that could be spent in more productive and satisfying endeavors. This story illustrates the application of this concept brilliantly.

A concierge working in a baroque, historic hotel helped a guest with directions to a Gray Line Tour bus pickup point. Unfortunately, the guest could not follow the directions given, missed *the bus and decided to vent at the concierge. The guest suggested that the hotel should post signs explaining how to get to the tour pickup area. (Admittedly, this is an absurd thought. Imagine taking it to its literal conclusion — signs for every direction someone might ask for). The concierge **reacted** instead of acting or responding. He did not take the few seconds necessary to assess the situation and realize the guest needed to be right. Instead he began to explain to the guest **why** they couldn't possibly put up signs explaining the location of the Gray Line tour pickup — "Because the lobby was historic and the aesthetic would be ruined." The guest was not satisfied with this response, as it completely dismissed his frustration. The guest and the concierge continued to belabor this point, believe it or not, for twenty minutes! That was nineteen and one-half minutes longer than the situation warranted. If the concierge had **"Being Right Is the Booby Prize,"** in his brain, he could have simply **agreed** with the guest, used a great listening technique and written down the suggestion, apologized for any inconvenience, rebooked the tour and appreciated his suggestion.*

*The exchange would have taken just a few moments if the concierge had responded with, "What a great idea," instead of spending twenty minutes in a feeding frenzy, fighting for the right to be **right**. Everyone would have emerged a winner, and the concierge would have had nineteen extra minutes to be more productive.*

Because being right is so hair-trigger automatic, it is possible to start out with being right, catch yourself, and get back on the "all-win" track. Being aware of the "Neon Signs" will help you catch yourself in the act of "Being Right." You start by "Staying in Touch with the Challenge." Then "Choose." The following story illustrates this perfectly.

The airport shuttle driver approached me to announce his departure without our guest, who had a reservation. I asked him to please wait another few minutes. I combed the lobby calling his name and rang his room to no avail. Finally, eight minutes after the scheduled departure time I let the shuttle driver leave. Four minutes later the guest appeared in a huge huff demanding to know what happened to his airport transportation. Wanting to be right and filled with the confidence that I was right, I proceeded to tell him how I had called out his name and he was **not** in the lobby. He huffed and he puffed and said he was indeed in the lobby. It was at that moment that I thought, Oops! Give it up! My **"Neon Sign"** flashed **"Stay in Touch with the Challenge,"** — This man needs a ride to the airport.

Another flash: **"Choose."** I quickly switched gears. **"Being Right Is the Booby Prize."** I apologized. I had obviously missed him. I took action and arranged other transportation quickly. What positive outcome could possibly have occurred if I had held on to being right? The answer, of course, is **none.** This process can save you a great deal of aggravation.

A cocktail server participating in one of my seminars relayed this story:

A particularly rude group of customers had been heckling her for over one hour, making lewd comments and generally treating her disrespectfully. Obviously unconscious that their behavior was offensive, they asked her to take a photo of the group. She gladly and willingly complied, all too delighted to frame the photo so their heads would not appear in the frame. Momentary revenge? Indeed! The server had the instantaneous, and short-lived pleasure of getting even, and being right. In the long run, everybody lost.

Remember, you can choose to be right or you can choose to serve. Keep these "Neon Signs of Service" uppermost in your mind and you'll be a happier customer-service provider as well as a happier human being. David Roth, a wonderful singer-songwriter, wrote a song called, "Would You Rather Be Happy or Right?" You know those cranky customers? Chances are, they'll seem a little mellower as well.

"Stay in Touch with the Challenge"

"Choose"

"Being Right Is the Booby Prize"

EXERCISE: Think about a time in your own work when you had to be right. What happened? Was the customer satisfied? Were their wants and needs taken care of? How did you feel? What pushes your buttons enough to make you want to be right? You can use the following worksheet.

EXAMPLE: One seminar participant said his buttons really get pushed when someone "throws" a credit card at him. Another participant, hearing this, said, 'Oh, I love that! I act as if I'm going for a jump shot." Once you are aware of what pushes your buttons, you can make conscious choices.

Check it out for yourself. Notice the difference in energy expenditure in the time and effort it takes to be right in relationship to the ultimate outcome. I think you'll agree that it is in your own best interest to give up the need to be right and go with the flow. It's the art of service.

**Examples of situations that push your buttons
(and cause you to use your favorite way to be right):**

_____

_____

_____

_____

_____

_____

_____

_____

_____

How could you think of them as alarm buttons and use the technique?

Notice it is occurring. Name what is happening. Choose.

_____

_____

_____

_____

_____

_____

THE NEON SIGNS OF SERVICE

Getting to the Heart of the Matter in Customer Service

Look for the Love

What's love got to do with it? Everything!

The first time I decided to speak about love in a business setting, I was nervous and apprehensive. The more I've talked about love in the workplace, the more comfortable I've become. I've realized that "Looking for the Love" is a highly productive strategy for service providers, and more importantly, I am not alone. This is a universal truth that applies to everyone and everything.

Bringing more love into your work is both the best offense and the best defense when faced with difficult people and situations.

I was conducting a seminar at the New York, New York Hotel in Las Vegas when I wandered into a store called the Motown Café. I was immediately drawn to a purse that was designed to look like a 3-dimensional stop sign, and it had the name of that famous Motown song, "Stop In The Name of Love" emblazoned across it. I had to have it as prop for my seminars. I love visual aids. It made me laugh and helps people remember this powerful "Neon Sign."

You see, in order to look for the love, you have to stop your immediate negative emotional trigger. You have to stop in the name of love when faced with an unhappy customer, and see them as a person who has problems and challenges, laughter and sorrow, ups and downs in life, just like you do. <u>They are someone's mother or father, son or daughter, husband or wife. Using this Neon Sign, "Look for the Love," prevents service providers from becoming victims.</u>

I learned this strategy early on in my career as a concierge. I was having a very pleasant exchange with two lovely gentlemen who were interested in information on tours of San Francisco. We were engaged in conversation when I noticed that two women were approaching the desk, like two dark clouds!

*I wanted to complete the conversation with the two gentlemen so I would be free to concentrate on these women, who looked like they were going to be a challenge. As the women got closer to my desk they stood behind these nice men, and I quickly realized these arrogant ladies were their **wives.** One gentleman turned to his wife and explained that we had been talking about tours. No sooner did he say the word tour, than I heard fingers snapping in my face and in a disgusted and horrified tone came the words "Tours, heavens no! **You!!** (fingers snapping), get **me** a limousine."*

My "Neon Signs" were flashing:
First, "Deal with the Double D's,"
Then "It Isn't Personal,"
followed by "Choose."

*In that split second, I chose to **"Look for the Love,"** to be in the essence of my job and not just the function. The function, of course, was to get a limousine. I knew how to do that and was taking the appropriate action steps to get that part of the job done. The choice in this case was to not only handle the function, but to be in the essence of service, to be aware of the human needs and not just the business needs.*

*While calling for the limousine, I engaged my left brain and silently challenged myself. "Find something about this woman to love," was my mantra. Trust me, this was a challenge! Yet I was determined **not** to be a victim of her nastiness. I forced myself to imagine that people actually loved her. She was obviously*

married to a nice guy, and she was most likely someone's daughter, aunt, cousin, sister, friend, and mother. I kept repeating over and over to myself, "Someone loves this person, find something about her to love."

Just when I was sure the limousine was about to arrive and I'd failed to find something, I noticed a bracelet on her left wrist. Eureka! Pay dirt! I was familiar with the design. However, because I believe that there are moments when **"Lights, Camera, Action"** *is most appropriate, I pretended I had never seen a bracelet like that before. I asked her very politely if I could see the bracelet a bit closer, as I wanted to see what it said. I commented on its beauty as I spoke aloud what the bracelet spelled out in diamonds on her wrist, "I LOVE YOU."*

The negative vibes that had been present moments earlier immediately vanished. The energy around the desk completely changed. The limousine arrived and off they went, leaving me to help the next customer in a positive, service-oriented way. By taking the high road, forcing myself to **"Look for the Love,"** *I emerged the winner, for I was not a victim of someone else's negativity.*

I can assure you I earned a huge "Psychic Salary" that day. If I had not chosen to "Look for the Love," resentment would have taken over and my service spirit would have been cracked, if not momentarily broken. Worse yet, the next customer I helped would have become a victim (through me) of her nastiness as well.

I t is up to you. You get to choose, moment-by-moment-by-moment. Service is about love. It is not just about giving love to your customers. *It's about loving yourself in return. It is about taking care of yourself so you have what it takes to take care of others.*

THE NEON SIGNS OF SERVICE

Getting to the Heart of the Matter in Customer Service

Breathe and Stretch

Taking care of yourself so you have what it takes to take care of others is paramount for service providers. You have what it takes to do the job or you would not have been hired. What it takes to continue is self-renewal. That's the heart of this "Neon Sign."

I consider myself an expert on the subject of self-nurturing. I was 18 when my father recognized my affinity for "self-care." He proclaimed that I would never have to worry because *no* one would ever take better care of *me* than *me*. How prophetic that was.

I was only 22 when he died. Broken-hearted, I began a path of self-discovery that led me to healers and teachers running the gamut from acupuncture to Zen Buddhism. I've earned my reputation among

my friends as the queen of self-improvement! So, while I may lack a university Ph.D. in this topic, I feel highly qualified to share the expertise gleaned while earning my very personal "Doctorate of Self-Care."

Many people that serve others for a living have a deep-seated need to be needed, and have an easier time giving than receiving. It takes a shift in thinking to realize that giving to yourself is the best thing you can possibly do to be even more available to give to others. The single most powerful investment you can make is an investment in yourself!

Let's face it. Delivering front-line customer service is stressful. A customer can show up, behave rudely and later that manifests in your body as, literally, a pain in the neck. Swollen feet and ankles result from standing for long periods of time and gastrointestinal problems are natural by-products of the hectic schedules service providers lead, as many try to juggle their jobs with home responsibilities, and school as well.

You must take time to care for yourself or the well will eventually run dry and everything will suffer. While there are thousands of books, tapes, and classes that promote this concept, I am including it in a book about customer service because I firmly believe that this "Neon Sign" is an invaluable tool for service providers.

This isn't about eating fruits and vegetables and drinking eight glasses of water a day, although that's very good advice. Do it! My mission is to get you to make taking a moment for yourself a priority. I'm saying "a moment" because I'm sensitive, empathetic and realistic about those of you who are parents with small children, coupled with having demanding jobs. You may not be able to take two hours to go the gym. I just met a woman who is up at 4:30 a.m. and gets home at 8 p.m. — with no kids. Kids or no kids, you can take five or ten minutes, even if it is in the car, before you handle the next item on your agenda.

During my concierge years, when I just couldn't handle another question, I would take a very quick break, run down to the kitchen, tear into the freezer, close the door and scream at the top of my lungs. Hey, it was safe. No one could hear me in there and the temperature cooled down my body heat as well! Very refreshed, and only moments later, I returned to the front line able to serve once again.

Breathing

This "Neon Sign" is double-sided. One side is for the present moment. That is, on the job, recognize when you're feeling stressed. Take a moment. Go to the restroom. Go to the freezer. Walk around the block. The simplest way to nurture yourself is through breathing. It may sound silly, but when people are busy, their breath becomes shallow and labored. Taking a few moments to breathe deeply is the quickest, most effective, least expensive and most readily available stress relief.

Breathe slowly and deeply with your hands on your diaphragm, count five breaths in and five breaths out, repeat three times. This can be done at red lights, or in the car before you enter your house after work. Do this breathing with your tongue at the roof of your mouth for an even quicker relaxation.

Find a safe place to breathe at work; just remember not to do your deep breathing in front of the customers.

*During one of my early consulting jobs I was teaching the concierge staff at a very elegant hotel in Hawaii. I taught them a very quick stress relief technique — taking three deep breaths. I did not, however, heed my own advice and practice the special Neon Sign of "**Make No Assumptions.**" I assumed that everyone would know not to breathe deeply in front of the customers. A few months later I received a call from the hotel's general manager. It seems the concierge was serving a very difficult guest and felt the need to use the three deep breaths stress-relief technique. Rather than waiting until she could leave her post, she simply said to the guest, "Just a minute, I have to breathe!" With that, she pushed her chair back and proceeded to take three deep breaths and then said, "I can help you now." When the rather astonished and difficult guest complained about this behavior, the response of the concierge was that I, the expert consultant, had taught her the technique.*

So I'm making it clear here: Don't do the deep breathing in front of the customer.

Here is another very effective breathing technique that, for obvious reasons, needs to be done in private.

Alternative Hemisphere Breathing — Sit or stand with your spine straight. Rest the right thumb on the right nostril, the ring finger on the left nostril, and exhale through both nostrils. Now, hold the right nostril closed with your right thumb. Slowly and deeply inhale through the left nostril to a count of five. Keeping the right

nostril closed, press the left nostril closed and count to five. Now, open the right nostril only and exhale to a count of five. Without pausing, inhale through the right nostril to a count of five. Press both nostrils closed and hold for a count of five. Open the left nostril and exhale through it for five counts. Repeat five to ten times.

In over 20 years of searching, seminars, healers and self-care exploration, the following technique is the most efficient and effective tool I have ever encountered.

Most, of us, especially when we are busy, have all of our energy spinning around in our heads. We have become detached from our bodies and become scattered and fragmented. To take a moment to re-group and ground quickly changes the energy and, most importantly, gives you the ability to be in touch with your intuition and your higher self.

The following "Grounding and Centering" process was created by Aimee Lyndon-Adams, a very talented teacher of energetic healing, as well as quality customer service. When I first learned it, I considered it to be one of the best gifts I had ever received. I do this every day at least two times and depending on the circumstance, I repeat the process as many times as necessary. (Once at a large party I was hosting, I excused myself several times — got grounded — and returned. Otherwise, I was so excited and hyped up that I knew the time would fly by and I wouldn't remember the event. Grounding kept me present so I could enjoy the party and all the memories.)

A simple process for Grounding and Centering — Sit with your legs uncrossed, with your feet about a foot apart. Place your hands palm down on your thighs and gently close your eyes.

Shift your awareness to the base of the spine. Take a deep breath (in through the nose) and as you slowly exhale (out through the mouth with a "ha" sound) imagine that you are sending a cord from the base of your spine all the way down to the center of the

earth. The exhale is twice as long as the inhale. Return your awareness to the base of the spine and breathe that cord down again, this time making it 50% thicker and stronger.

Return your awareness to the base of the spine and this time, as you take another deep breath, exhale a cord down each of the legs and out through the bottoms of the feet all the way down to the center of the earth.

The center of the earth is red, hot and molten. Using a pumping breath (in through the nose and out through the mouth, but this time the breaths are equal in length), imagine each time you exhale that you are drawing the earth energy up into your feet and ankles. You may start to feel a warm and tingling sensation as you continue to bring it up into the knees and thighs — filling every cell with revitalizing earth energy. Draw the earth energy up until it reaches the base of your spine and notice how it continues to rise up of its own accord filling every cell of your body with earth energy.

Now, to protect your energy field, just like the ozone layer is designed to protect the earth, take a deep grounding breath and imagine placing a layer of protective blue energy all around you. Start above the top of your head and sweep it down in front of you, underneath your feet and back up behind you, rejoining above the top of your head. Then sweep another layer down both sides. The final layer is to make sure there are no gaps or holes in your field of protection.

Feel how it feels to be grounded and centered. Imprint it, so that when you stop feeling this way you will be reminded to redo your grounding and centering. The more you practice this, the more you will develop the circuitry, and eventually you can ground in one breath.

I recommend that you do this practice twice a day in the privacy of your home — once in the morning and once at night. As you become proficient with practice, you will easily be able to reestablish your grounding and centering during the day, by taking a deep breath and bringing your awareness down to your abdomen (your center); and by taking another deep breath and imagining your own personal ozone layer safely protecting you. You will feel refreshed and ready to meet the challenges of the day.

Grounding is the ability to be fully present and responsive while being able to access all of your options. When you are not grounded vision closes down and you become reactive.

Movement

The next best stress reliever and self-renewal strategy is movement. Except for creating a rhythm and dancing through the day, this one usually falls on the other side of this "Neon Sign," — the one that you do off the job, and that usually takes more time. Exercise, stretching, dancing, moving — there is nothing better to break up muscle knots. I'm an advocate of massages and spas, but they are nothing more than a Band-Aid compared to the lasting effects daily movement can deliver. The best exercise is the one you will actually do, so choose one that nurtures you. Swimming, spinning, biking, hiking, walking, running, aerobics, yoga, hip-hop. Whatever it is, promise you'll do it and keep your promise.

When it comes to self-nurturing activities, the issue is almost always time-oriented. Let's look at this a moment. I believe it's not simply about the time — it is about your attitude regarding time, and not the time itself. Look at your behavior and notice if you seem to always make time for others, but not for yourself.

A great technique to overcome this tendency is to schedule time for yourself. I'm serious. Write it in your planner, make an appointment with yourself and don't break it. If you absolutely can't find time during the day, then this solution is for you. Make your day longer by waking up 15 minutes earlier than usual, and those 15 minutes are for you only! You must plan your nurturing, because most people don't give themselves permission to be nurtured.

Also, I encourage you to set boundaries. Practicing "The Wings of No" in one's personal life works as well as it does in business. Many people are afraid to say "no" to a friend, spouse or child for fear of not being needed. It is worthwhile to observe your behavior to see if this is true for you. Saying "yes" when you want to say "no" is a perfect way to sabotage self-renewal. Saying "no" helps to set the boundaries necessary for your own nurturing.

The most successful way to discover what would nurture you is to ask yourself this question. *What did I love to do as a child?* What were my favorite games, my favorite playtime activities? Once you have answered that question, ask yourself, "Is there anything I did as a child that I can do as an adult?" If there is, make a declaration and commit to doing it. A declaration is important. Tell a supportive friend, and have them hold you to it. The spoken word is very powerful.

Asking the question "what did I love to do as a child" saved my life. At one point in my concierge career, I was so stressed out, I was sure I would pass out in the middle of a shift. I knew I had to do something to bring balance and self-renewal into my life. I asked the question regarding childhood play and three things came to mind — ice skating, bike riding and swimming. Living in San Francisco, the ice rink situation was rather scarce and the abundance of hills made the bicycle-riding idea limited in appeal. So I gave swimming a try. I have been swimming regularly for 20 years! Now it is a priority in my life, as it is gentle and nurturing.

When I swim I think of it as time for *me*. I even call it "My swim, I'm going to take my swim." I never say "I'm going swimming." I also never count laps. It is not about counting or competition. It is about relaxing and moving and enjoying! Swimming opens my mind. While

I'm in the water, I figure out what I'm packing for my next trip, I write speeches, or I sometimes ask a question I want an answer to and swim with a knowing that the answer will come. Taking the time to take care of myself renews me, and provides me with the juice I need to serve my clients, friends and family.

Renew Yourself

There are so many ways to renew yourself. My seminar participants have shared hundreds of ideas. Here are a few ideas for things you can do easily, without even leaving the house:

- ❤ Play your favorite music and dance to it.
- ❤ Take a hot bath with aroma oils.
- ❤ Read a book.
- ❤ Putter in the garden.
- ❤ Arrange flowers.
- ❤ Meditate.

Don't answer the phone just because it rings — let the answering machine get it. Lock your door and camp out in the silence. The obvious benefit is that you slowly become a human being instead of just a human doing! (Shopping and going out to dinner are nice, but they are not truly about self-renewal. A walk in nature is more like it.)

If you're not taking care of yourself, you're even more vulnerable to self-sabotage. Beware of these six classic paths to self-sabotage and derail them with self-care!

1 - Monkey Mind. That's what Buddha called it. Have you heard that nasty little devil voice lately? Say, in the last five minutes? He has one purpose and one purpose only, to make you doubt yourself. Self-esteem is such an important aspect of service; self-doubt is an enemy that must be dealt with quickly. Make friends with the devil voice. (I call mine "the man with the whip" and I send out squads of cheerleader voices to calm him down and stop the constant whip-cracking banter — "You're not good enough, you didn't do this well enough, you're not really smart," and on and on). It's funny on Saturday Night Live, but live in your head is

torture. This critical voice is the polar opposite of self-care. Learning to be a friend to yourself is not an overnight process. Acknowledge the voice, since it will never go away. However, you can make it smaller than the voice of your own personal cheerleader. Eventually the cheerleader will become the louder voice, and play a dominant role in stopping the monkey mind.

2 - Comparisons. Simply put, this is a one-way path to misery. It is a constant process to resist the temptation to compare yourself to others. I am a member of the National Speakers Association, a group of very outgoing, highly accomplished professionals. While I truly enjoy going to meetings and growing in my chosen profession, the hardest work for me is to be comfortable with myself and my own path, and not compare myself to everyone else. It isn't easy, but it's definitely worth working on because the alternative is so damaging and futile.

3 - Resisting the Good. This is so subtle, you may not even realize you are doing it. By not taking in compliments, you are rejecting your personal power. I was in the Seattle airport going up an escalator, and as the down escalator passed me, a lady called out, "Your hair is so pretty, what do you put on it?" I candidly replied "Chlorine." I surprised myself with such a curt response to an obviously kind compliment! I've since realized that I was sabotaging my own self-care by not allowing myself to accept a compliment.

4 - Unclear Boundaries. This is a trap many people-pleasers fall into. As mentioned earlier, try practicing "The Wings of No." Or, instead of immediately replying, give yourself some time. Say, "I'll get back to you," or "I have to check my calendar." Then you'll have time to consider whether it's something you could pass up. When you commit to doing something you really didn't want to do, the penalty is doubled. You're spending your time unwisely and you're mad at yourself as well.

5 - Not Asking for What You Want. Most people aren't psychic. You need to ask for the things you want. The very fact that you have asked for what you want is a step in the right direction. You always win when you are brave enough to take the risk to ask. If you don't ask, chances are you won't get it.

6 - Staying in Toxic Relationships. A toxic relationship is one where you always feel worse after you've been with the person than if you had never seen them at all. Sometimes families can be toxic. In that case, proceed with caution and set boundaries. Meaningful relationships are critical to well being.

Forgiveness is part of taking care of you.

Who's perfect? Striving for perfection destines you for a disappointing life. Why is it that although you manage to please customer after customer, the one person who "blows up" becomes the focus of your thoughts? I'm assuming this happens to you, too! It's certainly happened to me a lot. When I worked at the hotel, if I felt responsible for a customer's negative experience I obsessed about it for days. I don't know why we do this. Even now, I struggle with this issue. If I am giving a lecture and most of the room is attentive, but one person is sleeping or looking at their watch, I have to resist the urge to obsess about that one person. What's important is concentrating your energies on the people who are with you, and not being distracted by the negative disturbances that are bound to happen around you.

It's important to forgive yourself, for you can never be all things to all people. Forgiveness is only possible when you are actually doing the best that you possibly can. There is a great sense of freedom in doing one's best. It allows you to forgive imperfection and to concentrate on the things you did well.

Most service providers possess the nature to nurture. We simply need to nurture that nature.

The Neon Signs of Service
Getting to the Heart of the Matter in Customer Service

The Wings of No™

In a world where the only response people want to hear is "Yes," learning how to make "No" fly is a valuable skill. As a service provider, there are times when you must be the messenger of "No" tidings. Your customer is disappointed, unhappy, or downright rude. The flashing "ME" sign is saying "Give me what I want, now!" It is time for a bevy of Neon Signs to go to work: "Stay in Touch with the Challenge," "Choose," "Forgive," and "It's Not Personal."

Along with colloquialisms like, "The customer is always right," advertising doesn't help your customer's expectations. This is an actual quote from an ad I found in an airline magazine: "A staff that only says yes." Yikes! What a setup for staff and customers alike for over-promise and under-deliver.

Early in the creation of the concierge concept in the United States, Hyatt ran an ad that said in essence that the concierge never refuses any request. That ad came back to haunt us on several occasions. "What do you mean you won't come up to my room? It says right here in the *New York Times* that the concierge never refuses a request."

In service positions, no matter how much the advertising suggests otherwise, there are times when "yes" is not an option and "no" becomes a necessity.

Here are some examples from my seminars.

No • They don't have that time available.

No • This check cannot be cashed today.

No • We don't have the view room you requested available.

No • Your table isn't ready at the time of your reservation.

No • You can't park in the fire lane.

And on and on and on.

S aying "no," even in the most polite manner will never be as appreciated as getting the desired answer. Learning to make "no" fly will absolutely, beyond any question of a doubt, make "no" easier to accept. So, how do you make "no" fly? *Give it wings!*

The first wing is caring and the second wing is providing an alternative. "No" or the statement of limitation comes in the middle.

 **The Wings of No**

Statement of Caring   Statement of Limitation   Alternatives
"NO"

First of all understand that "no" is half a sentence. Most people who provide good service understand the concept of offering alternatives, and offering to find out information. That is one wing of "no."

Offering alternatives:

"We can't do this, we don't have that . . . Here is what we can do!" (Offer alternative).

The problem is that one wing is aerodynamically insufficient to actually fly. It takes two wings to fly. The first wing is needed to establish that you care about the customer and their problem and get into rapport with them. It can be anything from an apology (See the chapter on Art of the Apology) to a caring statement that lets the customer know you are truly interested in their well-being and in resolving the issue.

Here are some examples of caring statements:

"I can see how frustrating this must be for you."
"I wish there was more I could do to help."
"That must be so disappointing. I would really like to be able to help you."
"I can imagine how upsetting this is for you. I'd love to find a way to help."

It is not just the words you say that are important here. Your body language must support what you are saying. Examples of positive body language are leaning in, eye contact, and a warm voice tone. You negate your words by crossing your arms, stepping backwards, avoiding eye contact and talking with a hollow voice tone.

Caring is a way of showing the customer that you can put yourself in their shoes — perhaps they are tired, feeling inconvenienced, frustrated, they're having a terrible day and the current dilemma is the last straw. Caring builds rapport. It puts you in personal touch with the customer, so they feel that you are involved in their welfare and their experience. It is handling the feelings first.

It is vitally important because if you just say "no" first, people don't even hear the alternatives. Your sincere caring creates an openness to listening for the customer to hear what the options are. You can't possibly satisfy people if they think you don't care.

Obviously, this is easier said than done. Certainly there are times when it is challenging to care. Perhaps you know that the customer is not telling the truth. You told them the price or the hours and they are insisting that you didn't. What if you are not feeling well that day and can't relate to the customer's misery?

The bottom line is that if you want the situation to be the least stressful, use a caring statement anyway. If you don't, it's simply that much harder for you. That's why the Neon Signs can be so helpful.

They can help you keep your perspective and help you "Keep Dancing." Sometimes behavior has to come before attitude. While it is ideal for attitude to be first and behavior to follow, it may be necessary to act "as if" and the attitude will follow. Try it. The results may put a smile on your face.

While caring softens the times when you have to say "no," it will not necessarily make the customer ecstatic or thrilled that they cannot receive what they are wanting. It will, however, make the situation more palatable, easier to handle, and the message easier to deliver and receive.

So whatever you do, don't skip this first step. Many people use the second wing of providing alternatives, but without the caring it does not make "no" fly.

Now, let's look at the second wing — providing alternatives. Coming up with other options reinforces that you care, and while it might not be the exact answer the customer wanted, it may actually solve the problem.

This requires creative thinking. You probably get similar customer requests — don't customers ask for the same or similar things over and over? It follows that you also know what you can and cannot provide, right? So taking the time to think through some alternatives, and keeping these ideas in your back pocket helps you to more quickly satisfy the customer and in turn, builds your confidence.

When you're using both wings — a statement of caring and a statement of limitation — it looks and sounds like this:

Question: "Can I bring my pet to the hotel?"
Caring Statement: (First Wing) "I love to travel with my pet." I understand how important that is.
Statement of Limitation: "We are not able to have pets stay in the hotel."

> **Alternative: (Second Wing)** "There's a kennel very close by, and if you would like I can call them for you or give you the phone number, whichever you prefer."

A caring statement I've used successfully goes like this: "You have no idea how much I want to tell you exactly what you want to hear. [PAUSE] And, tonight, I'm simply not able to. Instead, I'd like to offer you _____."

It's very easy and natural to use the word, "but." Watch yourself on this and make a concerted effort to eliminate the "but" word from your vocabulary. Substitute the word "and." The word "and" makes it possible to have two conflicting thoughts in the same sentence. This takes some practice, *and* it is a very valuable skill. The trick is to *pause* between the first wing of "no" and the word "and."

Example:

> "I wish I could accommodate your request. I know we have been able to in the past [PAUSE] *(the pause is vital)*
>
> *and* in this case I am unable to accommodate it. Let me tell you what I can do. . ."

My friend Jeanne Jenkins Perry, who was the first concierge on the Monterey Peninsula, learned early on that the **"ME"** sign was prevalent in all of her guests. Knowing that people want what they want when they want it, delivering bad news had to be developed as an art form.

If Jeanne had to let people know that the restaurant or car rental or hotel was not available at their chosen time, she always had an alternative. She used **"The Wings of No"** with a twist. When she told the customer the alternative, she whispered it! Not only did she whisper it, her body language was very powerful. She leaned forward, spoke exclusively to them, nodded her head and made it seem like the alternative was a big secret. It worked like a charm, every time!! She dubbed it "The Whisper That Works."

Example: "Lights, Camera, Action:"

*"I wish I could have booked you into Postrio; however, they were full at 8pm. **(Lean in, be exclusive, nod and whisper),** I was able to secure something at Bix at 8pm."* Customer responds, enthusiastically, *"Book it!"*
Jeanne really understood service as a performing art.

Practicing "The Wings of No" is very important because it can easily drift into the dangerous territory of *being right* and we have already established that "Being Right Is the Booby Prize." Consider this real-life example from a seminar participant.

A security officer in Texas needed to tell a truck driver that he couldn't enter a restricted zone that had been clearly signed. Her polite attempt at "The Wings of No" went like this:

"I'm sorry that you didn't see the sign, but I can't let you in here, you'll have to turn and loop around."

For a first stab at this concept, it is a step up from a flat-out, *"You can't enter here."* However it is still subtly saying, *"You're wrong, you should have read the sign,"* or, with the right body language, not so subtly saying, *"You're stupid, you didn't see the sign."* (Slap! Bad customer!)

"I apologize for the inconvenience."	"And, we no longer allow vehicles to drive in here."	"It will only take a minute to loop around. Thank you for your cooperation."

Service providers waste so much energy *being right!* Compare the first attempt to the following "Wings of No" for the same situation.

The difference is profound, it doesn't make anyone wrong, and the chances of someone *not* screeching away in a huff are substantially increased. Analyze the difference.

Wing 1: STATEMENT OF CARING

First attempt: "I'm sorry you didn't see the sign."

Second attempt: "I apologize for the inconvenience."

It is important to distinguish that we shouldn't have to apologize for doing our jobs. We can and should apologize for frustration or inconvenience. Many service providers balk at apologizing when they have done nothing wrong. Yet, research shows that almost everyone wants an apology. It's the right thing to do. Apologize for the fact that the customer has been inconvenienced. That is valid and authentic.

The STATEMENT OF LIMITATION

First attempt: "But I can't let you in here."

Second attempt: "And we no longer allow vehicles to drive in here."

The word "but" mitigates the apology; the word "and" continues it as a statement.

Wing 2: ALTERNATIVE STATEMENT

First attempt: "You'll have to loop around."

Second attempt: "It will only take you a minute to loop around. Thank you for your cooperation."

Telling people who are either upset or paying for a service that they *have to* do something alienates them. However elementary it may seem, "please" and "thank you" are timeless concepts.

Here's a good example:

Telling customers not to smoke in a restaurant is a challenge for restaurant employees. In California where it is a state law, the easiest thing to do is ask someone to put out the cigar or cigarette and quote the law or policy.

A better way to handle it is to use "The Wings of No" and not make the customer wrong and bad.

"I'm sorry to disturb you while you're enjoying a cigarette."	"And, perhaps you are not aware there is a regulation in California that all restaurants are smoke-free."	"We have provided a place on the patio where you may smoke."

It's easy to tell customers that the reason the answer is "no" is because it is the company policy. While policy can occasionally be quoted, it should never be the first thing you tell a customer.

Think of it this way. If you are the customer and you want something and the response you hear is, "It's not our policy," how do you feel? If you're anything like the thousands of customers I've spoken to, you'll be thinking, who cares about your policy — change it!!!

Quoting policy perturbs people and is guaranteed to annoy. So much of understanding service situations is in understanding psychology. It helps to think of it this way: The word "policy" sounds very strict. In our culture, we associate strictness with teachers and parents. When we feel we are being directed by a parent, it is natural to behave like a child. Service needs to be delivered by adults to adults.

I think of the word "policy" as the international No Parking sign. Don't use it unless it's the only way to explain it, and then lead into it rather than leading with it.

EXERCISE:

While many of the techniques in the book can easily become natural responses to situations, this particular one is a learned skill that takes practice.

Come up with a list of occasions where you have to tell the customer "no" in your business.

Then, for each one, find out if everyone is aware of the alternatives available for the problem presented. If not, brainstorm alternatives.

Then, practice via role playing saying "no" without offending people.

CAVEAT: In situations where there are no alternatives to offer, you need to offer a sincere apology.

"The Wings of No" was conceived in collaboration with Dana Gribben.

THE NEON SIGNS OF SERVICE
Getting to the Heart of the Matter in Customer Service

Apologize

Have you ever heard or thought, "If they had just apologized, I would have been satisfied"? Most people are reasonable as long as you let them know you *care*. As long as people feel that someone is paying some attention to them, and showing concern for their situation, ruffled feathers can usually be smoothed.

When they're not, the consequences can be costly. This story was reported in a June 1999 issue of *People Magazine:*

Annoyed by a telemarketer, a resident of West Virginia asked the person on the phone to take her name off the list, and not to call again. Two weeks later when she was called again, she wrote to complain. Three months later, she was contacted again. Frustrated, she sued the company in small claims court for violating the telephone Consumer Protection Act and sought $5,000 in damages. The company counter-sued charging that she had illegally recorded their calls. The judge threw out the counter-suit and required the company to pay $4,000 and apologize for suing her. She received the payment but not the apology. She sued again, this time for $45,000. The case was settled out of court.

Remember this "Neon Sign." Flash it. "Apologize."

Learning to apologize is one of the most disarming and useful concepts to employ when working with people. These acronyms are used frequently in the hospitality industry to teach employees the proper way to apologize. They are applicable to all industries.

L Listen		**H** Hear Them Out
E Empathize		**E** Empathize
A Apologize	**L** Listen	**A** Apologize
R Respond	**A** Apologize	**T** Take Action
N Notify	**S** Solve	
	T Thank	

The most important thing to remember when a customer is angry is to deal with the feelings first and solve the problem second. Because service is basically a feeling (a perception), you must always handle the feelings first. Before you can deal with the customer's feelings, you need to handle your own feelings. Remember to "Notice, Name, and Choose."

Because so many customers that require an apology are angry, a strategy I recommend is to hold up the Neon Sign, "Forgive." In the moment, forgive this customer for their behavior, humble yourself to serve and by doing so, you have raised yourself up so high above their behavior that you will not be affected by it.

This way you can serve the customer as a person and not get all confused with your reactions, emotions and feelings. So, person first, then the situation. Ask questions, so you are not on the defensive. This will help to diffuse people's anger and solve the problem. Asking questions forces people to make a decision. By giving alternatives, people have to stop, make a choice and respond.

> **If, for example, a guest's room is not ready until 3 p.m. and the guest has arrived at 12 noon you could say: "I can arrange a tour for you, or you can have a meal in our dining room. Which would you prefer?"**

The prime ingredients when serving upset customers are care, a sincere apology, and sincere empathizing. It is important to preserve a customer's self-esteem. If people feel understood and valued, it is infinitely easier to take the action required to solve the problem and move on to the next agenda item.

Whenever possible, the goal needs to be to turn around the customer. Make it a personal challenge to change an angry customer into at least a very satisfied one.

My friend Lorley Musiol in Las Vegas has a special award called "The Turn-Around Award." Whenever her staff turns a customer from an angry one to a satisfied one, they document it. They also have a doll strategically placed in the back office, and they physically turn the doll around. Each turn is worth prizes. The focus on turning the customer around has helped morale, and given the staff a renewed perspective on their job purpose.

For the times when the Neon Sign, "Apologize" flashes, I created this screen to use as a guide in working with upset customers. I call it:

"How to Get an 'A' in Customer Service."

A - Awareness
A - Acknowledgement
A - Agree
A - Apologize
A - Action
A - Appreciate
A - Amenity*

The first two steps are for you. Stay aware. "Stay in Touch with the Challenge." Acknowledge the feelings involved and move on to handle the customer's frustration. I have put this formula to very good use many, many times, and can attest to its effectiveness.

---

* Amenities are only available in certain industries such as restaurants and hotels, i.e., complimentary dinner, dessert, room night, etc.

*I was consulting at a resort property in Colorado when a customer had asked the concierge to book a golf tee time, which she did. When the customer arrived at the golf course, there was no reservation. Livid, he huffed and puffed up a steep hill for the sole purpose of venting. I was chosen as the object of his ventilation and I was prepared. I simply flashed the Neon Sign in my brain, **"Apologize."***

*And, **"Lights, Camera, Action."** I began:*

*"I **agree** with you, this is terrible, I can't imagine how frustrated you must be.*

*I **apologize** for this; we have ruined your morning and I am sorry.*

*Let me call the golf course and see when they can fit you in. **(action)***

*I **appreciate** that you came back here to tell us, so we can avoid this happening again."*

Most people will repeat their venting three times. This case was no exception. I kept using the formula, but changed the words. Eventually the customer was satisfied because this formula leaves no loopholes.

If you have truly dealt with your feelings, their feelings and tried your best to resolve the problem, relax — that is all you can do.

The magic apology formula covers the business needs as well as the human needs of listening, acknowledging and respecting people. CAVEAT: Whatever you do, don't become a robot. The formula is a guideline. You must create the verbiage that sounds organic to you. If you sound robotic, you sound patronizing and if you sound patronizing, you have defeated the purpose of the apology.

If the customer is abusive, here are some helpful things to say:
• "I know you are angry at the company/situation. This is the first time we are having this conversation so please help me, so I can help you."
• "I really want to help you, [PAUSE] and I am not able to while you are speaking to me in this manner."

Do not say, "Calm down!"(Have you ever noticed someone calmed down because you told them to?)

If you are the person responsible for the customer being angry, apologize and admit you made an error.

If you are not the person responsible, apologize anyway! Use the tenets in "How to Get an A in Customer Service" as a guide.

EXERCISE:
List three things you might have to apologize for at work.
• Make one a legitimate issue where you or the company was at fault.
• Make one a time that it was not your fault, but you took the heat for something you didn't cause, i.e., a co-worker or another department was responsible.
• Make one something that you feel is the customer's problem, not yours or your company's issue and yet the customer is very upset by the situation.

Now practice with a friend or co-worker by pulling up the screen "How to Get an A in Customer Service" and using the tools in this chapter. Develop wording that is comfortable and organic to you personally to address each of the above situations. It is important to practice this, as apologizing when it is not your fault is unnatural. This is a skill, and like all skills, it takes practice.

THE NEON SIGNS OF SERVICE
Getting to the Heart of the Matter in Customer Service

Keep Dancing

Imagine this: My associate, Michael Welch and I were sitting at our concierge desk on a fairly slow day when suddenly a tour bus pulled up and a sea of humanity poured into our lobby. Michael turned to me and as he stood up, leaned over and whispered in my ear, "Let's disco concierge."

I've never forgotten that! What a wonderful response to a potentially overwhelming and stressful situation. I was on my feet in a moment, dancing with an imaginary rhythm in my step, handling the hectic pace with a smile on my face. The results of making the conscious choice to dance through this challenge were astounding. There was no stress and we were having fun! We were in control and most importantly, guests were served in the most positive way possible.

Since then I've flashed the Neon Sign, "Keep Dancing," in many a daunting moment. Even more importantly, this concept brought to my awareness the existence of a rhythm, both the personal rhythm of individuals and the rhythm that's created in the workplace. I'm not talking about drumming or toe-tapping here. I'm talking about an energy that's created when you're in the flow of your work, whether it's typing at a computer or assembling a computer, delivering food to the table or creating it in the kitchen.

Most people are unaware of this rhythm. It is absolutely unconscious. It was for me until Michael showed me how to disco through that rush. The greatest benefit of being in touch with your own rhythm is that you can retrieve it once it's been broken. I can promise you, if you work with people, your rhythm will be broken! If you don't know you have a rhythm in the first place, how are you going to get it back once it's been broken? If you're conscious of it, you can retrieve it and continue with the work at hand, whether it's a customer you're serving or a proposal you're writing.

One time I called my friend Steve Bagley at the Willard Hotel in Washington D.C. He was very busy and rather than responding to my call in a stressful way, he simply said, "I'm dancing. Can I call you back?" Steve had taken one of my classes years ago and I was delighted to hear him putting this Neon Sign to good use!

In a restaurant with an open kitchen you can observe the chefs dancing their way through food preparation as they orchestrate the many elements of cooking your dinner. Whether it's one chef coordinating all the components that will go on your plate, or a team working together, it's magical to observe this rhythm in action.

Another great place to observe this phenomenon is at any renowned, service-oriented Nordstrom Department Store. When Nordstrom first opened in San Francisco I was privileged to work with their concierge staff in a consulting capacity. The only convenient time for the classes was early in the morning before the store opened. I arrived at the employee entrance at 8 a.m. and was surprised and delighted to hear rock and roll music cheerfully blasting over loudspeakers throughout the store. When I asked about it, I was told it was played to "set the pace."

As a matter of fact, just as I was finishing the manuscript for this book, I read in the newspapers that disc jockeys are the newest trend in retail establishments, from London to New York.

The benefits for customers, as well as service providers, of being in touch with your personal rhythm continue to astound me. It is such a positive approach to stressful situations in the workplace.

A friend of mine had a doctor's appointment at a very busy clinic — so busy that there were two receptionists handling the patients at the entry point. One of the doctors was delayed in surgery so all of the appointments had to be rearranged.

My friend was fascinated by the behavior of the two receptionists in the exact same situation. One handled it with compassion and style while the other was overwhelmed and rude. My friend asked the busy, yet helpful of the duo what her secret was. She said she gets into the "rhythm" of the situation and dances through it. Dancing or miserable, you make the choice.

Recently, this concept was reinforced through another unlikely source — my garbage man.

I was leaving my house to run an errand but the garbage truck was blocking my car. The garbage man waved to me and I assumed it was about moving out of the way. Then I realized he was waving because he wanted to say "Hello" to me. This intrigued me, so I went over to him and struck up a conversation. I asked him how he maintained such a positive attitude while picking up garbage. His response was simple and powerful. He said, "Misery is optional." Probing further, I asked him how he got through hours of picking up garbage every day while choosing to remain positive. He said he gets into a rhythm and turns it into a dance. Then he proceeded to show me his dance routine using a garbage can as his dance partner — picking up the "partner," placing it on the electric truck, waving his arm like Baryshnikov as he lifts up his partner, turning her over (i.e., dumping out the trash) and gently placing her on the ground again. I was mesmerized by Gene's dance and once again validated that the concept of dancing through your day really works! (Thank you Gene for your inspiration.) If it works for garbage, it will work for anything! It's all your choice. Remember Gene's warning words, "Misery is optional."

You might have overheard some of these typical expressions for describing a busy workplace (you may even have uttered them yourself!) "We're being slammed . . . we're in the weeds. . . we're drowning . . . we're being buried."

Each of these expressions creates an environment teeming with negativity. If service is essentially a feeling and a perception, and I believe that it is, what, pray tell, is the feeling and perception that is created from being slammed, in the weeds, drowning or buried? Customers *feel* these things. Compare the negative feelings created from the above statements to the positive feelings created by "Keep Dancing."

The benefits of being in touch with your own rhythm go far beyond getting service providers through a *crunch* time. This understanding can quite literally keep a bad moment exactly that, a bad moment, and not turn it into a bad day, resulting in starting over tomorrow and wasting hundreds of opportunities to shine.

I have often thought that the Neon Sign, "Keep Dancing," would be very helpful for checkers at grocery stores.

> Last year this concept was affirmed at Whole Foods Market. I was standing in line observing the checker who was obviously performing his job totally connected to his personal rhythm. He kept moving in semicircles and his hands seemed to be bouncing an imaginary ball. The checker at the next stand noticed and asked what he was doing. He replied, "The Bouncy dance." He continued by saying, "It helps me pass the last hour before I get to leave. You should try it, it works!"

During my years of sharing this concept with service providers, it's come to my attention that not everyone could relate to the metaphor of dancing. If you can relate to dancing through your day, great! If not, make up your own metaphor to describe your individual rhythm. It doesn't matter what it is, it only matters that you have a rhythm and are aware of it.

A metaphor is an image that suggests something else. For instance, if I say to a person, "You are a nut," it does not mean that they are actually a nut. The nut is just the metaphor. A metaphor is used to understand one element of experience in terms of another. When I say, "The man is a lion," I am using the image of a lion to draw attention to his lion-like characteristics.

Metaphor is a medium for understanding and communicating. It is a tool for creating sense in the world around us. While metaphors create common language, they can have nuances that are different for each of us. We all use metaphors daily. If dancing is *not* a metaphor you can relate to, make up a descriptive metaphor that speaks to your personal experience. What are the ones you would use for how you do your job?

Here are some examples of metaphors that seminar participants have chosen for themselves.

- ❤ Smooth sailing / raging storm
- ❤ A maestro conducting a symphony / music out of key
- ❤ Salmon swimming upstream / hitting a dam
- ❤ Juggler / dropping the balls
- ❤ Smooth plane ride / turbulence

EXERCISE:

Once you have chosen the metaphor for yourself, both for the flow and for the stress, do this exercise.

1. Close your eyes.

2. Put yourself in your job.

3. Imagine yourself having your metaphor for a great day. You are *in* your flow. *Feel it!* Be in your great day rhythm. Now, imagine that suddenly something happens to break that flow. What is it? List the things that can break your rhythm and move you into your negative metaphor. Here are a few from my seminar participants: your computer goes down, an interruption, rude person, and a fire alarm.

Example: I am at work experiencing the flow and rhythm of a graceful dance. The phone rings while I am handling three other customers. I answer the phone politely and attempt to place the customer on hold when I hear a loud voice breaking my rhythm with the shriek, "I'm in my car." Snap! My rhythm is broken; in my graceful dance, I became a frozen statue. Because I am aware of my dance, I am able to recover quickly, keep the feeling and perception upbeat, and continue working with a good attitude.

How to recover from a broken rhythm.
1. Close your eyes and now imagine yourself in your job experiencing your metaphor for your worst day. Feel it! Be in the broken rhythm.

For example: From smooth sailing to gale force winds.

Is there anything that can happen that could move you back into the flow of your metaphor for a good day? Perhaps:
- ❤ A few minutes alone
- ❤ A break
- ❤ Walking around the block
- ❤ Deep breaths
- ❤ Recalling a compliment
- ❤ A Neon Sign

Is there anything you can do or have done in the past to break the bad day rhythm?

Why is this information about our personal rhythm valuable? Because knowledge equals control. Knowledge is power. This new level of knowledge will help you "Choose." Understanding rhythm saves time and helps you adjust quicker. Most importantly, the customer and you, the service provider, are served from this understanding.

Help yourself to remember. Give yourself reminders to trigger you to move into the flow of your good day metaphor.

- ❤ Put a dot on your watch
- ❤ Place a piece of crystal in a strategic place
- ❤ Place a sticky note in a conspicuous place, like on your computer, or in a cash drawer

Use your imagination and change it often. Studies show that we stop noticing pithy statements very quickly after we hang them up. It is part of your job to constantly make sure you are aware of the entire picture.

While the ideas are simple, implementing quality service is complex and multifaceted. The following story truly shows that it's important to do *whatever* it takes to maintain your rhythm. Interestingly, I totally forgot about this incident until I found a red wig in my closet nine years after the fact.

WHEN A DEEP BREATH IS NOT ENOUGH

I was dancing. I was dancing so fast that I was losing my rhythm and tripping over my own feet. I had been a concierge for 12 years, this was my sixth consecutive shift, and I had not had a break for seven hours. I knew I had to go for a walk, get some air, take a deep breath and regroup, or I was going to lose it with a customer. I quickly signaled my partner Maryann that I *had* to walk away. She muttered "hurry up." And off I ran taking deep breaths and counting to ten. Deep breaths and counting to ten quickly changes the physiology in your brain — that is why it is so often suggested.

I walked to the corner and turned left. I was in the heart of the Union Square shopping district in San Francisco. The deep breathing and fresh air were not having the expected effect. I envisioned Maryann alone at the desk, and still my mind kept screaming, "I can't face going back yet." One more block I thought, and that will do it. I continued the breathing and walking to no avail. I had been gone six minutes.

All of a sudden my awareness went to a second floor window where I noticed a wig shop display. I bounded up the stairs, pulled a perky looking red wig off a styrofoam head, and popped it on my head! Wow! I was a new person! The clerk must have thought I was nuts. A couple of bobby pins to secure it, I paid for it and I was on my way — a new woman!!!

It worked! Maryann laughed so hard when she saw me that her mood changed as well. We both completed the shift in very good humor. Our clients as well as the two of us were positively served.

Am I suggesting we all become redheads? Not exactly. However, if you do work primarily on the phone, try it! I am suggesting that you go inside and do whatever it takes to get the job done. In this case, pretending I was a different person on the outside helped me go inside to muster up the required energy to complete my shift. It always happens from the inside out — not the outside in.

Marjorie Silverman came up with a fabulous idea that had her whole team dancing at the Westin Hotel in Chicago. During a particularly slow period in the middle of winter, she challenged the bellmen and doormen to write a song, which they did — brilliantly.

The project consumed weeks and got the whole crew through the slump and back into the busy season. They also worked it up as a show and performed it many times at hotel functions. She claims that it was the best team builder ever. The chorus goes:

We are the Westin Suitcase Crew
Schleppin' those bags,
Doin' it for you.

Why stiff us
When we're so good
Need help with your bags?
We knew you would.

You know we're not just working for fun
We're trying to make a living
Like everyone.

So, when you check in
You'll have no trouble
'Cause we're just here
To do the Suitcase Shuffle.

Now, that's dancing!

THE NEON SIGNS OF SERVICE

Getting to the Heart of the Matter in Customer Service

Lights, Camera, Action

It's showtime! If everyone in the service industry would adapt this theme, life *would be* more like a theme park. Now that is somewhat of an exaggeration (and maybe not desirable in some aspects), and it's not revolutionary or new. Nonetheless, it is important, especially in its essence.

Disney does it. Every park and hotel employee at a Disney property has been trained to be on stage, in a costume, as part of a cast, performing with a changing audience. Let's be clear about this — that includes every person behind a counter, at a ticket gate, or tending the grounds, not just the people performing on a stage. In uniform, they are in costume. At work, they are on stage.

Life in the lobby of the Grand Hyatt in San Francisco was, indeed a stage, and my concierge uniform, my costume. I chose to look at it that way. In some cases, my lines were well rehearsed (more about that in a moment). In others, they were unequivocally unrehearsed. As the audience changed, so did the names and characters in the play. What a fun concept . . . if you're *willing!*

I have to encourage you as a customer service provider to develop acting skills. Look for an acting class, an improv class ideally. Sign up for it and enjoy it. It will set the tone for you. You'll learn how to be spontaneous, in the moment. That's what it's all about ... being in the moment within a framework. At work, that's the customer's framework — it's his or her play. You are an actor. As you become more adept at this, you will move up into the director's chair. It becomes your play, as well. Now there's real power in that! The "Neon Signs" will help you be in control.

One of the best life lessons I've ever learned happened at age 24. I was living in New York City and my life felt like it had all of the components of a great drama — grief, romance, intrigue, danger; every-

thing appeared to be in the hands of other people. I went to a lecture at Lincoln Center one Sunday morning and the lesson I learned that day totally changed the way I looked at my life. The speaker said, "Do any of you think your life resembles a movie?" I could certainly relate to that! What he said next stunned me. "When are you going to realize you are the projector, *not* the screen." It is the same in every service job. You are in control — the producer, the director, and the actor. This is service as a performing art.

What, you might be asking, does this have to do with my job? Well, how about repetitious jobs, repetitious answers? Many service jobs are repetitious. Answering the same question over and over again with the same answer. Over and over again. Over and over again. Did you get that?

Do you realize that actors get paid (in money *and* psychic salaries) for doing the same thing over and over again? Their dream has come true when they get a "regular" job in a play on Broadway or anywhere, for that matter, and they get to do the same thing over and over again. Carol Channing in *Hello Dolly* repeatedly sang the same songs and said the same lines every day and night for years, all the while *acting* as if it was the first time she had said it.

When asked how she was able to do that, she replied, "Why, that's my job. The people listening have never heard me sing it before, so my job is to sing it like I never sang it before."

I cannot count the times I told people how to get to the cable cars from our hotel. It had to be thousands going on millions. It was a three-line answer. Over and over again. Flashing the Neon Sign, "Lights, Camera, Action," put me in the performance mode. I challenged myself to say it like I'd never said it before. I allowed myself to be in the moment with the customer. I'm not going to be delusional here and claim that I accomplished this all of the time. I'm advising you that it works, when you work it. It can make a good day better. This is for you, as well as the customer. This is customer service from the inside out.

It is a classic case of rewarding yourself with a "Psychic Salary." The function of the job is to deliver the information. The essence of the job is to deliver it like you've never said it before, for you, and your customer!

By embracing the concept of acting, you have a better chance of handling situations that annoy you with greater ease. This is definitely a case where service providers need to go inside and choose. Your manager is not going to be a cheerleader and say, "I know you can tell people where the cable car is like you never said it before" — (or whatever your repetitious statement). That has to come from inside you, because you're on stage.

Now here's an interesting phenomenon I've noticed. Most people in service jobs have resigned themselves to the repetition and are truly not rattled or disturbed in any way when they have to deliver the same information to different people. However, when they have to repeat the same information to the same person several times, it is universally disturbing, i.e., irritating.

The mind says, "Didn't I just tell you that?"

This is the perfect time to bring out the neon signs, "Stay in Touch with the Challenge," "Choose," and then "Lights, Camera, Action." You're on! It's your stage. Simply pretend it is someone else. You are in control of what annoys you, and this stuff is just too small to be irritating. It's your job. It's a moment in time. Let's make it light. Give it life. Give it your best. Give them a break and give it leverage.

Now, not everyone agrees with me about this. Some say that "acting" is phony — it's fake. While I agree the best service is sincere service, when that is not possible, acting is absolutely the next best thing.

Let's put this in perspective. What was the last live concert you attended? Before you went to that concert or show did you give any thought to how the performers were feeling? Did you care if they slept well, or had a fight with their spouse? Of course not! You paid your money and you expected them to perform for you. Customers are the same. They truly don't care about your personal life. They simply want what they want when they want it. There are no discounts for damaged goods or "seconds" in customer service. If you have a headache, cramps or a hangover, you'll have to rise above it, never lowering your delivery of service. Service never goes on sale because of how you feel.

Oscar Wilde put it this way: "Once you have mastered sincerity, you have acting down." It is a worthwhile skill to master.

The Neon Signs of Service
Getting to the Heart of the Matter in Customer Service

Bring Your Sense of Humor to Work

The transforming power of humor has been well documented in recent years, most notably for its role in people's recovery from serious illnesses. In my value system, the front line of customer service takes the prize for the next most important application of a sense of humor. *Looking* for the humor in situations and making a concerted effort to *find* the funny is vital for creating and maintaining an atmosphere and attitude that is service-oriented.

I considered my humor journal the most powerful tool in my toolbox when I worked on the front line, and ultimately it provided the cornerstone for my career as a professional speaker and trainer in customer service. I could never have made up the kind of stories I lived through on a day-to-day basis!

It's important to understand that "Bringing Your Sense of Humor to Work" is your choice. The only difference between comedians/comediennes and you is in how you look at life. You may read the newspaper or listen to the news and comment on how negative it all seems. Comedians read a newspaper and see the humor. The same item you shuddered at, late-night comedians (or their writers) put in a different perspective, and the world laughs at it in their monologues. Is it possible for someone who is not a comedy writer to find the humor in situations?

Absolutely! It's all in how you *look* at it.

Developing a humor consciousness takes practice. First, you must be *willing* to look at things differently. Decide that you're going to look for the funny by looking through the eyes of humor, and guess what? This is fun! It only takes two tools — a pen and notebook — teamed up with an *attitude.* You are now armed for creating a humor journal and adding levity to the workplace.

I *always* kept a small notebook at my concierge desk. I always bought one with a red cover and so I very cleverly called it the Red Book. Having this book is imperative to the process, because it's important to write incidents down as they occur. The problem with not keeping a journal is that funny things happen, but they get lost in the hubbub — sadly forgotten. The humor journal will not only help you remember, it sets you up to look for the funny. Mine became so treasured that I would measure the success of my day by how many entries I had in my humor journal — another way to pay myself a "Psychic Salary!" Keeping a humor journal also helps you "Keep Dancing" in the face of those things that break your rhythm. When you're looking for the humor, you'll be having too much fun to be distracted.

Once you have your journal, you need to get into the habit of using it and this takes *practice*. It may also require some motivation. If adding levity and laughter to the workplace isn't enough incentive, try rewarding yourself or your staff with a prize for the best journal entry of the month! Read them aloud and share the joy!

Do whatever it takes to continually find the humor in life. It takes commitment and consistency to look for the magic in the face of adversity. The results are well worth it in the happier and more hilarious environment you'll be creating both for yourself and those around you!

At a seminar in Maine, a participant told me that a very famous store in that state actually fired employees for keeping a humor journal. Their theory was that a journal promoted laughing at customers, a concept they would not tolerate. I would never advocate laughing *at* customers. However, my experience taught me that learning to laugh is the best survival tool available. It's about laughing at the situation, and laughing at ourselves.

I remember a seminar attendee telling me that she got very annoyed by customers constantly saying, "Excuse me, do you work here?" It was a toy store and when they popped the question, she was high up on a ladder in an orange vest with the store logo on it! I suggested that she bring her sense of humor to work and find the funny in that situation instead. Why be annoyed when you could be amused? It's up to you.

This concept became crystal clear to me when I was helping a family visiting California from New York. They had been in California for several days and let me know that they were sick and tired of California food and wanted New York–style food. I responded by recommending a restaurant that I knew had a branch in New York. I suggested they dine at the Palm. Without skipping a beat they responded, "The Palm? What would we want that for? We have that in New York."

I loved it! At that exact moment I had a choice in how I would respond. The Neon Sign, "Choose," flashed! Just think, I could have said: "That's what you just asked me for," while gritting my teeth. Instead, I was *armed* with my little Red Book, my humor journal. I chose to find the humor and suggest another restaurant. In truth, I wanted to leap across my desk and hug these people. I wanted to sincerely thank them for the great story! Rather than being annoyed, I felt terrific. It was a great day because I got to write in my humor journal (and got some great material for storytelling, another bonus of keeping a journal). Bringing your sense of humor to work is also another great way to earn your "Psychic Salary!"

Paying attention to the humor relieves tension. Entries can run the gamut from stories, to one-liners, to incredible moments. Here is one of those:

During a hurricane at a southern Florida hotel, the evacuation process was in full swing. It was a very tense time — buses were waiting outside to remove the hotel guests and staff, the emergency sirens were blaring.
A guest called the desk and asked, "Would this be a good day to gather shells at the beach?"

Hello?!?! A natural response would have been to be annoyed or think this question too absurd to answer. I'm not sure I could have been as sharp as this hotel employee, who answered, "Madam, tell you what, why don't you open your balcony door, wait a few minutes, and they'll come to you!" By choosing to bring a sense of humor to work, the response the hotel employee gave was priceless.

I want to share with you my very favorite thing that ever happened during my concierge career — and without my humor journal, I could never have handled this the way I did.

A guy with a giant "ME" sign came storming through everybody. I was working with three people in front of me, two telephone calls on hold. This guy is wearing a "ME" sign so big, I couldn't believe it. He stormed right up to the desk, and very gruffly and assertively said, "Hey lady, I need a room for tonight."

I thought, "Hmm, okay," He didn't look like one of our guests, so I didn't want to send him to the front desk, so I said, "Sir, exactly what do you need?"

He said, "Well, I haven't slept in four days. I got three dollars. So where you gonna send me?"

Not wanting to upset the other guests, I acted ("Lights, Camera, Action") like it was normal. I took out maps and Hi-liters. I wanted to handle the situation with dignity. I was feeling very good. I sent him to the closest shelter. Everything was great. I paid myself my "Psychic Salary" that night!

Three days later, I looked up and there he was again! He looked at me and he said, "Hey lady, do you remember that shelter that you sent me to?"

I said, "Well, yes." And he said, "Well, I didn't like it. What else ya got?"

I'm thinking, "Only in San Francisco, would the homeless use a concierge, and then come back to complain!"

> Write it down! These stories are just too good to risk losing! When you work with people, there are always stories. Pay attention and make writing them down a priority.

Humor Is a Choice

All industries can benefit from keeping a humor journal. The following are a few samples from actual humor journals of my fellow hotel employees:

The "Where can I get . . . ?"

A tattooing machine

Antique stock certificates

Ox gallstones

Large variety of videos in Hindu at a store with wheelchair access

A Case of Not Being Understood

Question	Answer
Yuen E. Ted?	United Airlines
Where can I buy a Louis Von Newton bag?	Louis Vuitton
Good Cheese?	Gucci

The worst scenario of not being understood was this disaster:

A guest asked me how to get to Fremont, a small city in the Bay Area. So I sent him on the train to Fremont. Much to my dismay, I later discovered that he had actually wanted the Fairmont Hotel, only three blocks away from the Hyatt on Union Square!

Sure I know that . . .

"Do you know that you are in a draft here?"

"Is the post office open on Christmas?"

When making brunch reservations, a lady asked me, "How long does it take to eat?"

Sure enough

A guest asked me if a high satire would be above her daughter's head. The child was four.

A guest stole the hotel's towels and then sent them down to receiving to have us wrap them for him and send them to his home.

"Where can I get a quick divorce and married in the same day?"

While doing research for a speech I was presenting for the banking industry a banker in Seattle relayed the following story:

> *A customer came to the teller's window attempting to deposit a $10,000 check. The teller explained that a check that large needed approval from an officer. The customer was upset and confused and when the teller left to get the approval, the customer stormed out of the bank. This, of course, left the teller rather confused herself. About one hour later, the customer returned. This time, however, a policeman accompanied her. She walked back to the same teller and said, "What kind of approval do you need? Here's the officer!"*

Start your own humor journal! It is stress management in its highest form. I'd love to hear about your humor journal entries. Please pass along your funny stories by sending them to me via:

FAX   or   **E-mail to:**
(415) 383-1503   **thankyouinc@aol.com**

Sometimes it's a challenge to find the funny, but well worth the effort. Without this life-saving strategy, I could never have survived front-line service. I suggest you find supportive friends who can help you find the funny in everyday life. Use your imagination and don't ever forget to "Bring Your Sense of Humor to Work!"

THE NEON SIGNS OF SERVICE
Getting to the Heart of the Matter in Customer Service

Special Neon Signs

You're Not Going

No Little Pieces of Paper

Make No Assumptions

I wrote these "Neon Signs" specifically for the concierge. However, I believe they can be adapted to a variety of businesses. See if you can apply them to yours.

You're Not Going

I came up with "You're Not Going," to help new concierges with one of the most common requests they get. That is, "Where would you go for dinner?" Immediately, I teach the concierge to pull up the "Neon Sign" that says, "You're Not Going."

The truth is that the guest doesn't care where you would go. What they are really saying is, "Where should I go?" They want your response to be personal, which is why they phrase the question "personally."

It is important to understand this, so you don't make the mistake of suggesting a place (thing/decision) that would be right for you personally, but not necessarily the right place (thing/decision) for the customer.

Are there situations in your business that could benefit from the awareness that in customer service it's about the customer and not usually about the service provider's personal preferences?

A customer might ask, "What would you do?" "What route would you take?" "Which one would you choose?" Whose agenda is this? So many companies and service providers are unclear on this concept. Most everyone is stuck in their own agenda — either their own or the company's — not the customer's.

Remember, you're not choosing for you — you are choosing for them. The important thing for you to keep in mind is that it's about the customer. Empathize. Ask more questions to find out what they like, whether it's a restaurant, a vacation route or a sweater. Then share what you know and help them decide what it is *they* would really like.

no
LITTLE PIECES
OF PAPER

THE NEON SIGNS OF SERVICE
Getting to the Heart of the Matter in Customer Service

No Little Pieces of Paper

Believe it or not, this painstakingly simple and sensible concept is not commonly practiced. When I first wrote my textbook for the concierge profession, I hesitated to include this idea, as I was sure it was so simple and obvious that mentioning it would invite ridicule. How wrong I was! I am truly shocked that busy people with many tasks to accomplish do not have a system to log things. Instead, they write themselves notes on haphazard little pieces of paper (and then keep them for reference). These are easily lost, misplaced or overlooked, particularly when you are feeling overwhelmed.

*I did some consulting for an 850-room hotel. While the staff used log sheets for specific requests such as tours, limousines or restaurants, everything else was written on little pieces of paper. When I asked the manager about it, she said she has really **tried** to get the staff to use log sheets, but has been unsuccessful. I suggested removing the plastic holder filled with small pieces of white paper. Most managers don't even realize they are enabling the exact behavior they want to discourage.*

So, if you find yourself surrounded by little pieces of paper, pull up this Neon Sign, "No Little Pieces of Paper." Put the information in a logbook, notebook, file folder, or transfer it to a database. Get it in its proper place so you can find it again. If you won't need it again, throw it away! If applicable, a logbook is preferable because it gives you a running account of requests, and staff members from different shifts can easily reference it.

THE NEON SIGNS OF SERVICE
Getting to the Heart of the Matter in Customer Service

Make No Assumptions

It is so easy to assume that you know the answer to a question. As a human being, and as a person in a job situation where answering questions is very much a part of your job, you naturally want to answer questions promptly. Caution! This inclination leads to the tendency to make assumptions. While efficiency is good, making assumptions increases the risk of upsetting customers.

As a customer, it makes me absolutely crazy when service providers say, "I think," or "I believe," before giving an answer. Either it is or it isn't. Either you know or you don't. "I believe," or "I think," shows that you are making an assumption. When that tendency shows up, pull up the Neon Sign, "Make No Assumptions."

Better to say, "I don't know, and I'll find out for you shortly."

I learned the hard way to check and make sure my assumptions were correct. I once sent people to a restaurant I knew was open for lunch. When they got there the sign on the door said, "Closed for private party." My assumption created a bad experience for my customer. One simple phone call could have prevented it.

Here's another example:

A hotel worker in Baltimore was asked where the museum was. She answered with the directions to the museum. When the guest got there, it was closed. The guest asked for directions on a Monday. Instead of giving the directions, the proper response is, "Which day are you going?" Stay present, not rote.

Think before you answer. Check out what you *know*. Be *willing* to say, "I don't know. I will be happy to find out for you." Now you get the fun of discovery and coming back with an answer to someone's very good question, and the next time you will have the answer!

If service providers could only be *willing* to know that they don't know, front-line service would actually improve dramatically.

THE NEON SIGNS OF SERVICE
Getting to the Heart of the Matter in Customer Service

Thank You Very Much

If one thought sums up my customer service philosophy, it is in the power of seeing through the eyes of "Thank you very much." They're such common words, yet vastly underutilized. Sometimes they're uttered in passing, a common response to an everyday interchange. Other times, they're attached to lavish gifts, or an emotional exchange. They are also, too often, missing in action. "Thank you" is appreciation, acknowledgement, praise. When it's missing, the hole is gaping.

As a "Neon Sign," this one is quite simply the heartbeat of life in the customer service trenches. It was the very first "Neon Sign" I created. I think of it as the bookends for all of the "Neon Signs."

I don't know of a better story to illustrate the power of thank you than one that happened to me early in my professional career.

I grew up writing thank-you notes. It was one of those things my mother was a stickler about. (Thank you very much, Mom!) Sometimes I felt like she had me writing thank-you notes for thank-you notes. Any way you look at it, it was excellent training that has served me well.

In 1973, just two weeks before the school year was to begin, I was sitting in Cleveland, Ohio with my Masters Degree in Special Education, but no job. I decided to go directly to the top. I phoned Mr. Keith Gainey, the Superintendent of Public Schools Special Education Division for the Cleveland Public School System. I told him about my degree, and that quite frankly, I had no experience other than student teaching.

The most amazing thing happened. He placed me on hold and when he returned he asked me if I could meet with the principal of the Sunbeam School for Crippled Children that afternoon! I was delighted, but baffled. Why, with only two weeks to go before school started would the principal want to see me? It turned out that just that week the 7th-grade English and Social Studies teacher received a grant to go back to school to pursue a doctorate degree. The school risked losing funding if they did not fill his position with a person who had a Masters Degree with a major in the physically handicapped. I fit the bill!

That job was one of the best experiences I've ever had in my life. I loved my job and I greatly appreciated it, especially considering the circumstances and timing leading up to it, so I did what came naturally to me . . . I wrote Mr. Gainey a very simple but heartfelt thank-you note.

*The remarkable thing was his response. He called to tell me that in the 27 years he had been in education, **no one** had ever written him a thank-you note!!! I knew in that instant that I was **on to something.** If a simple thank you could mean that much to someone, why didn't more people do it?*

I began to pay attention to all the opportunities I had to thank people in my life, whether verbal, in writing, or through gifts or deeds. I also began to notice when people thanked me, and how important and uplifting that was to my spirit. I believe that in the giving and receiving of "Thank You Very Much," there's the opportunity for tremendous fullness in our lives. By paying attention and concentrating on "Thank You Very Much," my life became filled with it. That's quite a testimonial for a simple message. If you want to fill your life with "Thank You Very Much," start to be an advocate.

This concept brings me to the customer in customer service. A part of me wishes I could teach customer service to customers. Wouldn't it be great if customers were more aware of how important appreciation is to the service providers who are doing their best? With expectations from customers higher than ever, a thank you for a job well done goes a long, long way, and in all ways, makes sense for the customer as well.

I was taking a shuttle from Los Angeles to San Francisco. There had been bomb threats, so the atmosphere at the airport was very stressful. The airline had canceled several shuttle flights, so the lounge area was totally chaotic. The counter personnel were all relatively calm and doing a great job under enormous pressure. I was one of the victims of a cancelled flight. When I finally reached the counter, rather than opening with my needs, I stopped. I read the attendant's name tag, and started the conversation by using her name, complimenting her on the job she was doing, and empathizing with the difficulty of the situation. I got on the next flight to San Francisco (while many unhappy customers continued to be unhappy sitting in the lounge).

Now for a different customer approach . . .

I have a friend who works in Las Vegas, where the expectation on the part of customers is as unrealistic as the surroundings. A guest requested tickets to the four most popular shows in town. After much finagling she was able to obtain tickets for three out of four shows, and she suggested others to round out their evenings in town. Rather than showing any appreciation for the three shows she did obtain, the guest yelled at her and even went to the Director of Sales to complain. Ouch!

There is so much power in service. Service workers have the ability to make or break someone's experience by a sigh, a smile, a sneer, or a sincere thank you. And customers have the power to value service by complimenting service workers and offering a sincere thank you. When that doesn't happen, you have the power and control to carry on and refuse to let it break your spirit to serve, *if you choose.* It's your choice!

"Thank You Very Much" is also about praise. Positive reinforcement is absolutely necessary to sustain and maintain a high level of customer service. If people don't feel good about themselves, they will not be able to be good to others. This philosophy is so simple, and it is rooted in the four magic words of a happy and fulfilled life and business. "Thank You Very Much" is about acknowledging employees and customers on an ongoing basis and not just recognizing one employee a month. "Thank You Very Much" requires that we pay attention to the very basic and human elements that make up true service.

In a world of faceless, computerized, tape-machine communications, the need to thank and appreciate each other, the need to feel valued and important, and the craving to be appreciated is stronger than ever.

> **"Don't assume that managers know the best way to deal with people. Almost half of the managers tested did not understand that people repeat behavior that is rewarded. Almost 80% did not understand that the observations made in performance reviews should be specific rather than general."**
> **— Calab Atwood in** *Behavioral Sciences*

You don't have to *want* to praise people; you just have to do it if you want to be successful. One thing you can do to activate the power of "Thank You Very Much" in your life is to take a moment to stop and appreciate the service people you come in contact with every day. Here's an example: When you pick up your shoes from the shoemaker, don't just get your shoes, pay and leave. Take a moment, admire the craftsmanship, and tell the shoemaker that you appreciate his or her good work. Then pay. It only takes a moment, but the effect of that moment could be monumental to the shoemaker. Now imagine how several of those moments a day would feel like for you.

Think about how much it means to you when people behave in a rude or indifferent way as opposed to the customer who took the time, albeit briefly, to say "Thank you very much," or to be nice. On a recent trip to New York, I made a special effort to thank cab drivers for their courtesy in driving. I wondered if I was the only person who had done that all day.

It begins and ends with you. No one is going to sweep down on our society and turn it into a culture that nurtures and respects service providers. It is up to each of us to do our part to make that happen, both as a customer and as a service provider.

Employing the "Thank You Very Much" Neon Sign is a way to do that.

Some of you might be cynical right about now, thinking what is all this kindness stuff? "*I'm the customer, for heaven's sake, so why should I go out of my way to be appreciative and kind to the person waiting on me? I wait on people all day long, now it's my turn to be waited on. Why should I have to be responsible for the service I receive? It's up to companies to provide good service and acknowledge their employees. That's not my job.*"

This attitude is pervasive in our culture and what it really is, is a dead end. Quite simply and selfishly, if you want to get the best possible service, if you want to get what you desire, you will learn to be a good customer, and that starts with appreciation.

If you don't believe that your behavior has a direct effect on the service you receive just ask any counter person, hotel clerk, waitress or waiter, telephone representative, bank teller, hairdresser, dry cleaner, butcher, etc. The customer is part of the equation in the service relationship.

Every service relationship is a power relationship, and the important lesson to learn here is that the customer is not always the one wielding the power. All of us need to do our part to raise the service level in America. Making the Neon Sign "Thank You Very Much" an important part of your life as a customer and as a service provider will make a difference. It's a promise.

No appreciation on a regular basis drains enthusiasm and willingness. Forty million people wake up every day and ask, "May I help you?" yet we live in a society that places little value on service workers.

A quote from my book, "Thank You Very Much," says:

"People who serve aren't important.

   — Oh yeah?

What if we didn't show up for work one day?

THE WORLD WOULD STOP."

Here's to the millions of people who say, "May I help you?" every day, all day.

Now, get your rhythm going and let's wrap up the "Neon Signs" with this "Rap" song I wrote for one of my speeches:

Thank You Very Much

CHORUS:

Thank you very much, it's music to the ear

Thank you very much, it's what we need to hear

These four simple words, they will fill up your soul,

As saying "May I help you" can take a toll

I'm the clerk

I'm the waitress

I take orders by phone

I dry clean your clothes

I process your loan

These four simple words, what a difference they make

So say them and hear them for all of our sakes

Thank you very much

Welcome that sound

They do make a difference this much I've found

When you pay attention and look, really look

There's people, real people, the dishwasher and cook

A name tag, a uniform, not robots on a job

When you don't say thank you it's their spirits you rob

Please stop to acknowledge, take a moment to notice
It's a person not a program like WordPerfect or Lotus

Thank you very much, it's music to the ear
Thank you very much, it's what we need to hear

I sit at reception, I work for the airline
I bag, I guard, no office to call mine

Oh, but I make a difference
Take a look when you shop
Without service providers, the world it would stop
Please stop to say thank you
It just takes a minute
The blessings it carries bring joys that are infinite

So speak them and say them, but don't forget to receive
It's in the give and the take
That's the legacy we leave
To be kind, to be loving, to give to your fellow man
It's simple, it's easy and everyone can

Thank you very much, it's music to the ear
Thank you very much, it's what we need to hear

Holly Stiel – Biography

Holly Stiel is an internationally recognized expert on service, an author, professional speaker and seminar leader, dedicated to "teaching the art of customer service — from the inside out." She got her customer service training on the job during 17 years as a hotel concierge, serving up to 300 customers a day. She knows the agony and the ecstasy of customer service firsthand and believes that good service is an art form.

Holly single-handedly started the concierge department at San Francisco's Grand Hyatt and was the first American woman admitted to the exclusive international concierges' association, Les Clefs d'Or. She was a founding member of the association in the United States. In 1999, she was the first woman and non-corporate executive to receive the Distinguished Visiting Professor award from Johnson & Wales University.

In addition to "The Neon Signs of Service," she is the author of "Ultimate Service" — the definitive textbook for the concierge profession — and "Thank You Very Much," a book for anyone who has ever said, "May I help you?" A world-renowned leader in concierge service training, she has applied these skills to many other businesses outside the hospitality industry. The philosophies and skills for creating "Thank You Very Much" cultures in businesses and organizations are available through training programs called "Spirit in Service," available in multimedia formats, including video and DVD, through Stielmedia, LLC.

As a professional speaker, Holly has fascinated audiences of 3 to 3,000 with her anecdotes, wit, wisdom and grace in the United States, Canada, Asia, Mexico and South Africa. She is held in high esteem by those in her profession and has the respect and repeat business of many companies known for their high customer-service standards: Nordstrom, Bellagio Hotel & Resort, Motorola, Bank of America,

Compaq, Vail Associates and Pebble Beach Corporation, to name a few.

Holly is a self-taught expert on self-care, enthusiastically practicing what she preaches, a lifelong commitment (and program!) that she calls, "Taking Care of Yourself So You Have What It Takes to Take Care of Others."

Holly lives with and travels the world with her husband, world-class photographer Bill Apton. To see Bill's inspiring photos, visit his website at www.aptonphoto.com.

For more information, please go to www.thankyouverymuchinc.com.

Thank You Very Much, Inc.
728 Bay Rd.
Mill Valley, CA 94941

800-78-HOLLY
415-383-4220   Fax: 415-383-1503
thankyouinc@aol.com

Order Form

Quant.	Title	All Funds in U.S. dollars	Total
	THE NEON SIGNS OF SERVICE *"The content is outstanding. Holly's generous application of enthusiasm, sensitivity, intelligence and humor has made a real difference for our realtors in Canada."* —Peter Robinson, President and CEO, Coldwell Banker, Canada 6 by 9 inches, 152 pages	Unit price $20.00 Shipping within U.S.A. $5.00 To Canada & Mexico + $2.00 Overseas + $6.00	
	ULTIMATE SERVICE – The Complete Handbook to the World of the Concierge *"The book should also be read by everyone already in service positions."* —Marjorie Silverman, Chef Concierge, Hotel Intercontinental, Chicago 8.5 by 11 inches, 190 pages, spiral bound	Unit price $40.00 Shipping within U.S.A. $8.00 To Canada & Mexico + $3.00 Overseas + $9.00	
	THANK YOU VERY MUCH – A Book for Anyone Who Has Ever Said, "May I Help You?" *"A beautiful collection of inspirational quotes and timely thoughts on the true spirit and meaning of service."* — Stephen Covey, author of *The 7 Habits of Highly Effective People* 4 by 6.5 inches, 134 pages	Unit price $8.00 Shipping within U.S.A. $3.00 To Canada & Mexico + $2.00 Overseas + $4.00	
	GIVE STRESS A REST – Twenty top trainers, speakers and consultants share their insights and secrets for dramatically reducing stress so you can enjoy better health, confidence and relationships. Holly contributed a chapter entitled "Taking care of yourself so you have what it takes to take care of others." 9 by 6 inches, 256 pages	Unit price $20.00 Shipping within U.S.A. $5.00 To Canada & Mexico + $3.00 Overseas + $9.00	
	NEON SIGNS OF SERVICE Poster 18 by 24 inches, on glossy stock. Contains all 20 Neon Signs.	Unit Price $10.00 Shipping in tube $5.00 To Canada & Mexico + $2.00 Overseas + $4.00	
		Subtotal:	
		CA residents add 7% sales tax:	
	MAKE ALL CHECKS PAYABLE TO THANK YOU VERY MUCH, INC.	**Total:**	

Holly Stiel, professional speaker, author, trainer and consultant.

Teaching the art of customer service from the inside out.

Mail orders to: 728 Bay Road • Mill Valley, CA 94941

Phone or fax orders: (415) 383-4220 • Fax: (415) 383-1503

Please visit our website at www.thankyouverymuchinc.com

Order Form

Quant.	Title	All Funds in U.S. dollars	Total
	THE NEON SIGNS OF SERVICE *"The content is outstanding. Holly's generous application of enthusiasm, sensitivity, intelligence and humor has made a real difference for our realtors in Canada." —*Peter Robinson, President and CEO, Coldwell Banker, Canada 6 by 9 inches, 152 pages	Unit price $20.00 Shipping within U.S.A. $5.00 To Canada & Mexico + $2.00 Overseas + $6.00	
	ULTIMATE SERVICE – The Complete Handbook to the World of the Concierge *"The book should also be read by everyone already in service positions." —*Marjorie Silverman, Chef Concierge, Hotel Intercontinental, Chicago 8.5 by 11 inches, 190 pages, spiral bound	Unit price $40.00 Shipping within U.S.A. $8.00 To Canada & Mexico + $3.00 Overseas + $9.00	
	THANK YOU VERY MUCH – A Book for Anyone Who Has Ever Said, "May I Help You?" *"A beautiful collection of inspirational quotes and timely thoughts on the true spirit and meaning of service." —* Stephen Covey, author of *The 7 Habits of Highly Effective People* 4 by 6.5 inches, 134 pages	Unit price $8.00 Shipping within U.S.A. $3.00 To Canada & Mexico + $2.00 Overseas + $4.00	
	GIVE STRESS A REST – Twenty top trainers, speakers and consultants share their insights and secrets for dramatically reducing stress so you can enjoy better health, confidence and relationships. Holly contributed a chapter entitled "Taking care of yourself so you have what it takes to take care of others." 9 by 6 inches, 256 pages	Unit price $20.00 Shipping within U.S.A. $5.00 To Canada & Mexico + $3.00 Overseas + $9.00	
	NEON SIGNS OF SERVICE Poster 18 by 24 inches, on glossy stock. Contains all 20 Neon Signs.	Unit Price $10.00 Shipping in tube $5.00 To Canada & Mexico + $2.00 Overseas + $4.00	
		Subtotal:	
		CA residents add 7% sales tax:	
	MAKE ALL CHECKS PAYABLE TO THANK YOU VERY MUCH, INC.	**Total:**	

Holly Stiel, professional speaker, author, trainer and consultant.

Teaching the art of customer service from the inside out.

Mail orders to: 728 Bay Road • Mill Valley, CA 94941

Phone or fax orders: (415) 383-4220 • Fax: (415) 383-1503

Please visit our website at www.thankyouverymuchinc.com